Working with children
in care

Working with children in care:

European perspectives

Pat Petrie, Janet Boddy, Claire Cameron,
Valerie Wigfall and Antonia Simon

Open University Press

Open University Press
McGraw-Hill Education
McGraw-Hill House
Shoppenhangers Road
Maidenhead
Berkshire
England
SL6 2QL

email: enquiries@openup.co.uk
world wide web: www.openup.co.uk

and Two Penn Plaza, New York, NY 10121–2289, USA

First published 2006

A catalogue record of this book is available from the British Library.

ISBN–10: 0 335 216 34x (pb) 0335 216 358 (hb)
ISBN–13: 978 0335 216 345 (pb) 978 0335 216 352 (hb)

Library of Congress Cataloging-in-Publication Data
CIP data applied for

Typeset by YHT Ltd, London
Poland EU by OZGraf. S.A.
www.polskabook.pl.

The McGraw·Hill Companies

Contents

Acknowledgements

We would like to thank the Department of Health and the Department of Education and Skills for their support and funding of the work on which this book is based, while acknowledging that the views put forward are our own, not those of the Departments.

We are very much indebted to all the young people, children and workers (residential home staff, academics and other professionals) who participated in the research, and from whom we have learned so much. We are especially grateful to our research colleagues in continental Europe: Professor Marie Bie and Filip Coussée at the University of Ghent; Professors J. Van der Ploeg and E. Scholte at the University of Leiden; Professor Dr. Herbert Colla, Dr Thomas Gabriel, Rouven Meier, Tim Tausendfreund and Michael Tetzer at the University of Lüneburg; Professor Alain Bony of the Centre National Études et de Formation pour l'Enfance Inadaptée; M. Guy Dréano, formerly of Buc Ressources; Jytte Juul Jensen of the Jydsk Pædagog Seminarium, Århus; and Inge Danielsen at the Copenhagen Socialpædagogiske Seminarium.

We are most grateful to colleagues and former colleagues at the Thomas Coram Research Unit, Ellen Heptinstall and Susan McQuail for their valuable participation in planning the research and conducting fieldwork; to the data entry team – Nicoletta Cavriani, John Grey, Ilaria Geddes and Emilce Rees – and to Jaci Henry who worked on the references. We also offer our thanks to colleagues at the Thomas Coram Research Unit, in particular Peter Aggleton and Charlie Owen, for their insightful comments on the work, and Sharon Lawson for invaluable administrative support.

1 Introduction

Working with Children in Care: European Perspectives is written against the background of the gross social disadvantage suffered by children in the care of the state in England. The focus is on social pedagogy and an examination of what this distinctive approach, commonly used in continental Europe, has to offer the development of policy and practice towards such children, especially those who are looked after in residential establishments. It draws on the authors' research.

In this introductory chapter, we provide a brief outline of the field of social pedagogy in Europe; an overview of the main theoretical and policy perspectives on which we will draw; a short description of the research on which the book is based; and a summary of the chapters which follow.

We undertook the research, funded by the English Department of Health and the Department for Education and Skills, mainly because of concern about children who are 'looked after', and especially concern about those in residential care. The term 'looked after' was introduced by the Children Act, 1989, to refer to children and young people who are 'accommodated by the local authority' for more than 24 hours, either with parental agreement, subject to a Care Order passed by a Court, or at the request of the young person (over the age of 16). In the UK as a whole approximately 76,500 children and young people were looked after in local authority care in the year ending 31 March 2001 (National Statistics 2001), when we were starting our research.

These young people form a diverse group, but they share a multitude of disadvantages associated with life in the care system and are among the most socially excluded groups in our society (e.g., Department of Health 2000; Chase et al. 2002). For example, within education, looked after children are more likely to be excluded from school, to be non-attenders and to leave without qualifications (Jackson 1994; Social Exclusion Unit 1998; Department of Health 2000). They are more likely to be involved in criminal activity; there is a disproportionately high number of teenage conceptions among this group (Barnardo's 1996) and, on leaving care, they are at greater risk of unemployment and homelessness, relative to the general population (Biehal et al. 1995; Baldwin et al. 1997; Social Services Inspectorate 1997; Department of Health 2000). Recognition of these multiple disadvantages has resulted in the prioritization of their health, education and welfare in a number of government reports and initiatives. Of these young people, the majority (41,700) are placed with foster families, compared with 7000 in residential settings (National Statistics 2006). Yet, as we shall see, in many countries in continental Europe residential care is given a more prominent status, has been less a cause for concern and employs more highly qualified staff, specifically educated and trained as 'pedagogues'.

POLICY

TRAINING AND EDUCATION

PRACTICE

THEORY

Figure 1.1: Social pedagogy as an organic system

The concept and theory of pedagogy

We will discuss the term 'pedagogy' at much greater length in Chapter 2 and throughout this book. Here some preliminary definition of the term may be helpful. The concept of pedagogy is understood differently in the English-speaking world from the way it is understood in many European countries and the term *social pedagogy* is little used in English-speaking countries. Briefly, in continental Europe, pedagogy refers to children's upbringing, their education in the broadest sense of that word, while social pedagogy can refer to the whole domain of social responsibility for children, encompassing many types of provision. In the countries included in our studies of residential care, an organic pedagogic system could be distinguished (e.g., Petrie 2001). The system's components consist of policy and practice, theory and research, and the training and education of the workforce, with each component feeding into, and drawing from, the others [Figure 1.1].

Pedagogic theory is an academic field in its own right, and is the basis for education and training for staff working with children and young people in diverse settings, including residential care.

The domain of the pedagogue is not necessarily confined to work with children 'in need' or 'at risk'. Whatever the setting, educational, health, youth services, social services or nurseries, pedagogues usually work alongside other professionals and share the general aims of the establishment, but they bring their own distinctive principles, understandings and skills to bear. They may have a variety of job titles relating to the setting in which they work.

In Denmark, for example, pedagogues work as staff in nurseries, pre-schools, out-of-school services, children's residential establishments and in disability services with children or with adults. In spite of its etymological roots, we shall see that in much of Europe, those trained in pedagogy work with adults as well as children, for example in residential and day care, in community development and in family support.

Theoretical perspectives and concepts

Throughout this volume, we will present and discuss empirical data arising from our studies of pedagogy in Europe, undertaken on behalf of the Department of Health and the Department for Education and Skills. We will discuss our findings in the light of an interdisciplinary approach, based on our different backgrounds and interests as authors. These allow us to examine data from, and to make connections between, different theoretical and disciplinary perspectives.

Social exclusion and life chances

We begin our discussion of theoretical and conceptual issues by a brief consideration of two of the key concepts employed by the English government in describing their policy towards looked-after children. These concepts are 'social exclusion', and 'life chances', especially as they relate to education and employment as the key route out of poverty and its concomitants.

Since 1997, the UK government has expressed concern about people who are socially excluded, an understanding which includes children and young people in public care. In England, a Social Exclusion Unit (SEU) was established, in the Cabinet Office, and anti-exclusion measures have also been taken in Scotland, Wales and Northern Ireland. Social exclusion is a term that needs some unpacking. Although it is a recent coinage, the issues to which it relates are longstanding. Percy-Smith (2000: 1) describes its origins in the social policy of the French Socialist government in the 1980s, where it referred to people without access to social insurance. Subsequently, it was taken up by the European Union, to address regional disadvantage as a barrier to overall social and economic cohesion. Broadly speaking, social exclusion is used to describe the unequal social position of some members of the population: those people who have fewer resources, less access to services, lower social status and who participate less fully in the political and civic institutions of society. It is of course always used in a relative sense – these are people who are not in fact excluded from society, but they occupy a disadvantaged position within society, compared to more powerful groups.

> Social exclusion is a complex phenomenon. It is multi-dimensional, and can pass from generation to generation. Social exclusion includes poverty and low income, but is a broader concept and encompasses some of the wider causes and consequences of deprivation. The Government has defined social exclusion as: 'a shorthand term for what can happen when people or areas suffer from a combination of linked problems such as unemployment, poor skills, low incomes, unfair discrimination, poor housing, high crime, bad health and family breakdown.'
>
> (SEU 2004)

Percy-Smith and Byrne are among writers who draw attention to the inherently problematic nature of 'social exclusion' and claim the necessity of going beyond a shorthand definition. Byrne (1999: 128) argues that, generally, public policy in Europe, and even more so in the USA, sees social exclusion in a 'weak sense', as defined by Veit-Wilson (1998):

> In the 'weak' version of this discourse, the solutions lie in altering these excluded people's handicapping characteristics and enhancing their integration into dominant society. 'Stronger' forms of this discourse also emphasise the role of those who are doing the excluding and therefore aimed to solutions which reduced the powers of exclusion.
>
> (Veit-Wilson 1998: 45, cited by Byrne 1999: 5)

Morrow sees social exclusion and inclusion as examples of inherently pathologizing discourse (Morrow 1999: 761). Byrne (1999) has identified social exclusion as 'a necessary and inherent characteristic of an unequal post-industrial capitalism founded around a flexible labour market'. Percy-Smith, too, comments on the structural background to social exclusion. Referring to an earlier SEU document, she says that the term 'social exclusion' is sometimes taken as being more or less synonymous with poverty: 'This definition is very much focused on outcomes and makes no reference to the processes that create the problems identified in the definition' (Percy-Smith 2000: 4–5). She places social exclusion in the context of (i) the locality, particularities of place, population (all of which are implicated in the SEU 2004 definition) and local governance; (ii) national economic policy and welfare regime, rights of citizenship and responses to globalization; and (iii) in the wider context of globalization and associated structural changes – none of which are implicated in the SEU definition. All of these interactive contexts underlie processes that impact on children, looked-after or otherwise, and their advantaged/disadvantaged positions in society.

In connection with notions of social exclusion, the English government also employs the term 'life chances', a term used by the sociologist, Max Weber, relating to status and power, especially to economic power within the market, to social class and to access to a range of material goods, opportunities for income and other resources. The government in England applies the term to looked-after children, in alluding to their deprivation and its current and future outcomes. For example, the forward to an SEU report (SEU 2003: iii) says:

> the Government is committed to giving children in care all the same life chances any parent would give their child, and none is more important than a good education which is crucial to a brighter future. This sets major challenges. Being separated from family and friends, changing neighbourhoods and spending time out of school are difficult experiences for any child. Such an unsettling time makes it much harder to learn. It helps explain why almost half of children leave care with no qualifications at all. It is also a measurement of how society has failed these children in the past.

This extract acknowledges that the redress of disadvantage is outside the capability of the child, at the same time the parent of the looked-after child is rendered invisible. Here, 'any parent' – the normative parent – is seen as capable of providing children with 'life chances'. So what of the parents of children in care? These, it would seem, have not provided their children with life chances.

Children in care are, axiomatically, excluded from normative parenting – and the implication is that their parents, in their turn, are also so excluded. As the SEU report quoted above says, 'Social exclusion is a complex phenomenon. It is multi-dimensional, and can pass from generation to generation'. Here, the notion of social exclusion passing from generation to generation, without acknowledging the structural foundations of exclusion, is reduced to the level of the individual and their family inheritance. Socially excluded people are seen as caught in vicious spirals involving, over generations, the interplay of unemployment, poor education, poverty, bad housing, physical and mental health difficulties, addiction and criminality.

A strong emphasis in the English government's social inclusion policy is the promotion of employment, with education and qualification as the route into employment. For individuals and populations who have seemed more resistant to general education and employment measures, targeted welfare programmes and other initiatives come into play. For example, the *Sure Start* programmes in England, for pre-schoolers and their parents, combine health, educational approaches and parent support. The *Sure Start* initiative was intended to bring the advantages of education and employment to local disadvantaged populations. Similar intentions have underlain programmes such as the *Education Action Zones* and *Health Improvement Zones*.

When it comes to children in public care, the government has set a range of targets. The Department of Health's *Quality Protects* programme, launched in September 1998, laid down specific aims and set outcome targets for all aspects of children's lives, with the local authority as 'corporate parent' being responsible for the well-being and progress of the children in its care. Its objectives included ensuring that children looked after 'gain maximum life chance benefits from educational opportunities, health care and social care' and that young people leaving care, 'as they enter adulthood, are not isolated and participate socially and economically as citizens'. Local authorities are obliged to submit evidence, annually, that young people in care are meeting these objectives, with indicators relating to educational attainment, school attendance, offending rates and health care. Welfare provision targeted at disadvantaged groups is known as residual welfare, in contrast to universal welfare which is available to the whole population (Titmuss 1958). Esping-Anderson 1999: 40–1) refers to the extent to which social risk is evenly distributed across social strata. He comments that a residual approach divides society into 'them and us' with, on one side, a self-reliant majority of citizens and, on the other, a minoritarean and dependent welfare state clientele. In contrast, a universalistic approach is based on the solidarity of 'the people'.

Welfare regimes

The welfare regimes of the countries included in our studies were somewhat different from each other, as were the models of social work that they employed. It is important to consider these differences by way of preface to what follows. As Worning (2002) comments, welfare policy is not 'a distant theoretical abstraction. On the contrary, it can be felt in the body every day, because political prioritisation constantly changes conditions for the staff who have to provide welfare service to the citizens' (Worning 2002: 2). We would add that it also, importantly, changes conditions for looked-after children and for their families.

Esping-Andersen (1999), in an approach derived from classical European political economy, distinguishes three ideal types of welfare regime, each of which is represented among the countries studied. These three models are not uncontested (e.g., Pringle 1998; Abrahamson 2002), and Esping-Anderson has himself continued to develop them. Nevertheless, although they are broad ideal types, they provide a useful conceptual tool for social policy analysis. Welfare regime is here defined as the combined, interdependent way in which welfare is produced and allocated between state, market, family and the 'third sector' of voluntary, or non-profit, welfare delivery (Esping-Anderson 1999: 35).

England falls within the broad model of *neo-liberal* regimes, (with the USA offering a purer example). Neo-liberal regimes, sometimes referred to as the Anglo-Saxon model, seek to minimize the role of the state and to promote market solutions (Esping-Anderson 1999: 74–6) and 'third-way' partnerships between the private and public sector. Neo-liberal regimes see welfare in terms of 'picking up bad risks left behind by market failure' (Esping-Anderson 1999: 83). Targeted and special services are provided for those who present a social risk because the material and other resources of the family are insufficient. Within this model, England has seen welfare services – such as Sure Start – targeted at localities of high need. It has also seen the development of private care services, with residential care among the latest of children's services to be developed in the for-profit sector. While there is government regulation of children's welfare services, and policy to raise the standard of staff qualification, nevertheless, individual proprietors themselves set the requirements for their workforce.

The *social democratic* welfare regime is virtually synonymous with the Nordic countries and is also known as the Nordic model (Esping-Anderson 1999: 78–81). It is re-distributive in terms of wealth, with universal welfare and benefit systems used as of right. Universal welfare services are publicly provided, of right, as means of supporting active citizenship and social/economic participation. Staff in welfare services such as nurseries and children's residential establishments are required to be highly trained. The Nordic model depends upon a high level of employment, including female employment. The responsibilities of the family for the welfare of its members is less emphasized than in the other models, while the state assumes greater responsibility. 'To many, the egalitarian element is simply the practice of universalism: everybody enjoys the same rights and benefits whether rich or poor. To others, it refers to the active promotion of well-being and life chances. Still others equate egalitarianism with redistribution and the elimination of poverty' (Esping-Anderson 1999: 79–80).

Using the same welfare regime typology, Germany, Belgium and France all may be placed, broadly, in the *conservative* framework. Esping-Anderson (1999: 8) comments that labelling the continental European welfare states as conservative may appear pejorative, but his intention is to convey their dominant political thrust. In these systems, people in employment – and their families – are protected from risk by compulsory social insurance. There is social assistance for those who are neither supported by their families nor protected by employment and, therefore, by social insurance. As with the liberal approach, social assistance is stressed rather than the universal rights to benefits and welfare services of the Nordic model. In contrast to liberal regimes, there is very little private market provision. In the conservative model, welfare services – including those of children in care – are extensive, and often delivered by voluntary, including religious, organizations, supported by the State.

Theories of social work

It may also be useful, at this point, to draw attention to different theories of social work, in order properly to position social pedagogy, and to allow readers to see how, to some extent, they can map onto the three different types of welfare regime. Payne (2005) distinguishes three main theories of social work.

Individualistic-reformist theories focus on social work as a 'response to social and political demands for order' (Payne 2005: 13) and 'maintaining people during any difficulties they may be experiencing, so that they can recover stability again'. Payne remarks that this view of social work 'expresses the liberal or rational economic political philosophy – that personal freedom in economic markets, supported by the rule of law, is the best way of organising societies' (Payne 2005: 9). This resonates with Esping-Anderson's neo-liberal model. Payne also relates this individualistic-reformist theory of social work to more technical types of social work practice.

Payne sees *socialist-collectivist* theories as 'ideas within social work which focus on its social purposes. It [social work] is concerned with social change' (Payne 2005: 13). He says that they imply that disadvantaged and the oppressed people will never gain personal or social empowerment unless society is transformed, and relates this view of social work to socialist political philosophy – with planned economies and social provision promoting equality and social justice (in line with Esping-Anderson's social democratic model).

Reflexive-therapeutic theories of social work on the other hand represent, according to Payne, 'the ideas within social work which concern personal development and fulfilment, with an emphasis on emotions and inter-personal responses' (Payne 2005: 9). The term 'reflexive' is important here, implying that, through their interactions, social workers and their clients affect and change each other. Payne sees social pedagogy as 'the general theory of social work that concentrates on social work as an educational and developmental process' (Payne 2005: 51). He sees it as a practice in which 'individual and collective self-development and education interact' (Payne 2005: 209).

This approach finds a place in both the more paternalistic conservative welfare state model, and in the social democratic model. In so far as the UK exemplifies the neo-liberal approach, the UK model of social work/social care should perhaps be based more in individualistic-reformist approaches, and more technical types of social work practice. But, as Payne points out, in the UK all three theories of social work are represented, although some are more prominent in some institutions and settings than in others. We will examine our empirical findings to see how far results may best be interpreted in the light of these different models of welfare and of social work.

Residential care: the historical background

We turn now to one site for the practice of social work, namely residential care for children, and briefly outline something of its history. European countries included in the studies which we refer to in the course of this book, have a history of residential care that shows some similarities and noticeable differences. To some extent, the history of residential care has become a history of concern about residential care.

In many countries, while there had been some earlier forms of care for children outside their families of origin, a large expansion in residential institutions occurred alongside the processes and events often referred to as the industrial revolution. With the visible growth of the urbanized poor, with changes in the family economy and employment located predominantly outside the home, the position of children within the family and society changed.

Throughout the nineteenth century, a variety of residential institutions were brought into existence. Their purposes included removing destitute children from the streets, accommodating, educating, controlling and sometimes employing them, and in the case of delinquent children, reforming them. The twentieth century was to see a growing unease about the nature and extent of residential institutions. This stemmed from various sources. In part, there was concern about the conditions to be met in residential institutions for children in the public care, see, for example, the English Curtis Report (1946) and scandals such as those concerning child abuse in North Wales (Waterhouse 2000) and the use of 'pin down' – the excessive and punitive control of children (Staffordshire County Council 1991).

In addition, there was a growing distrust of institutions, and the institutionalization and stigma associated with them. The work of the sociologist Irving Goffman in the 1960s and 1970s was widely influential in this regard (e.g., Goffman 1961, 1963). In England, residential care developed from the Poor Law workhouse, with that institution's essentially stigmatizing and disadvantaging history: a history that suggests the potency of residential care for furthering the relative social exclusion of residents – unless, that is, such disadvantaging characteristics are addressed directly.

Writing of the evolution of French institutions, Dréano (1998: 291–2) draws attention to their prioritizing their own maintenance and preservation, their rigidity and 'egocentricism'. In Germany it has been suggested (Thomas 2000) that institutions were counterproductive in addressing children's therapeutic needs, compared to their more basic functions of providing food and shelter. Thomas notes that the recognition that 'labelling' is associated with living in institutions has led to the search for conceptual and practical alternatives. Madge observes that, generally in Europe, there have been:

> considerable changes in the residential care that remain in the circumstances under which children are placed. Provision has been tailored to a variety of needs, homes have become smaller and more personal, children stay for shorter periods, and much stronger links are maintained with the community.
>
> (Madge 1994: 50)

A preference for foster care, rather than residential care, as an alternative to a child's birth family can be attributed in large part to the influence of John Bowlby's psychoanalytic approach following the Second World War, and his views on the detrimental effects of the deprivation of an attachment figure (more specifically a mother figure) on young children (e.g., Bowlby 1951). Madge (1994) reports a general decline in residential care in favour of fostering in the countries which were members of the European Union, at the time of her study. Nevertheless, the proportions of children in residential care were, and continue to be, much lower in the United Kingdom than in other countries in the EU (Browne et al, 2006). This issue is discussed in more detail in Chapter 3, but nevertheless: 'An impression of greater optimism about residential child care is evident in many European countries relative to the United Kingdom. There may be problems but this does not detract from a certain "confidence" in the service itself' (Madge 1994: 137).

In a lecture given in 1970, Winnicott (1984: 225–7) proposed the essential features of *therapeutic* residential care, if further damage to children's development is to be avoided, and earlier damage made good. His work inspired the discussion of the contribution that psychotherapy can make to the treatment of children living in residential care (e.g., Sutton 1991), and to its potential in supporting staff and their practice (Briggs 2004). Yet it is striking how little discussion about the theories and concepts which might underpin the practice of residential care have taken place in England, outside more experimental and 'alternative' forms of provision.

Both Denmark and Germany, together with the other countries we have studied, have an important underlying theoretical framework for residential care: that of pedagogy, which theorizes and values the 'everyday' events and processes of residential life. But pedagogy is not the only theoretical resource to which practitioners in these countries can turn. Through their initial and ongoing training, pedagogues can access numerous, and eclectic, theoretical approaches to work with children and young people, and theoretical developments in psychiatry and psychology have been highly influential (Jensen 2000).

Theories of parenting and attachment

Our consideration of the relative benefits of pedagogy as an approach to work with looked-after children raises an over-arching conceptual question. To what extent is residential care work like parenting? This question seems particularly apposite in the context of English policy rhetoric about 'corporate parenting' (e.g., DfES 2003). Undeniably, the differences between parenting in a family environment and care work in a residential setting are profound. For example, while parents are ultimately responsible for the 'big' issues in children's lives – such as, where they live or go to school – residential care workers are not. Some will participate in these decisions for one or more of the children in their care, but the responsibility is shared by the child's social worker and other professionals, including, in England, the local elected council member as 'corporate parent', along with, for many children, the birth parents. Nevertheless there are similarities in that both parents and residential care workers have relationships with the children they look after, and responsibilities for their everyday care and day-to-day lives. Although this responsibility is shared across the staff group in a residential establishment, it nonetheless seems plausible that theories of parenting and parent–child relationships have relevance for an understanding of what residential provision sets out to achieve.

Attachment theory

Bowlby's attachment theory, and particularly his 1951 monograph for the World Health Organisation (WHO), has had a considerable impact on child care policies in England (Rutter and O'Connor 1999). Bowlby postulated that the key damaging feature of group residential care was the lack of personalized caregiving and hence the lack of opportunity to develop selective attachments, and indeed there is evidence of this from more recent research with infants in institutional care (Vorria et al. 2003). We have already noted that Bowlby's work influenced a fundamental aim that continues to guide policies for looked-after children in England today, and which underpins the English policy preference for foster care: to provide personalized caregiving in a family context and thus allow continuity in relationships. Here, our purpose is not to question this policy approach, nor to evaluate how well foster care provision succeeds in this regard. Rather, it remains to ask how the principles of attachment theory apply to the provision of residential care for young people who are looked after.

From a historical perspective, attachment theory differed from previous theories of personality development and psychopathology in emphasizing the importance of both continuity and sensitive responsivity in caregiving relationships. According to Rutter and O'Connor (1999: 824): 'Most crucially, [attachment theory] proposed that the development of selective attachments serves a purpose – namely, the provision of emotional security and protection against stress. This was a novel notion in the 1960s …' The function of attachment is thus to provide the individual with a secure relational base from which he or she can operate (Bowlby 1973). Beyond infancy, attachment relations come to be increasingly governed by internal (mental) working models that the individual constructs from experience. Bretherton and Munholland (1999: 91) observed that Bowlby (1973) conceived these as 'operable' models of the self and the attachment partner, based on their relationship history:

> A working model of the self as valued and competent, according to this view, is constructed in the context of a working model of parents as emotionally available, but also as supportive of exploratory activities. Conversely, a working model of self as devalued and incompetent is the counterpart of a working model of parents as rejecting or ignoring of attachment behaviour and/or interfering with exploration.

Ainsworth et al.'s (Ainsworth et al. 1978) account of attachment theory emphasized sensitive and responsive caregiving, and there is substantial evidence of the relationship between caregiver sensitivity and attachment security (e.g., Bakermans-Kranenburg et al. 2003). More recently, Meins (1999, cited in Howe 2005) has developed discussions of parental sensitivity with reference to what she terms 'mind-mindedness', namely: '[the] proclivity [of parents] to treat their infants as individuals with minds, rather than merely entities with needs that must be met' (Howe 2005: 20). According to

Meins and her colleagues (2002), the parent's attunement to the infant's mental state helps the child to become aware of his or her own and other people's mental states and processes, and how these govern behaviour. In this, parental mind-mindedness is associated both with attachment security and with children's developing social understanding, or 'theory of mind'.

In considering the relevance of these theories of parent–infant relations, for our understanding of work in residential care, there is a need to address two common misconceptions of attachment theory – first, that attachment is monotropic, and second, that it is a theory of infant development. While emphasizing the importance of the early mother–infant relationship, neither Bowlby nor Ainsworth contended that this is the only attachment relationship that an individual has, and indeed there is much evidence of the multiplicity of attachment relationships. Further, attachment theory is a lifespan developmental theory: attachments, and associated internal working models, are formed throughout life (see Cassidy and Shaver 1999, for an overview of the attachment literature). These points are particularly pertinent to work with children looked after, because there is evidence that key figures such as teachers and foster carers can provide compensatory attachment models for children and young people who have experienced adverse parenting (e.g., Howes and Ritchie 1999; Kretchmar et al. 2005).

Rutter and O'Connor (1999) remarked that while it is often assumed that the key risk of institutional provision is the lack of continuous personalized caregiving – and while indeed staff turnover remains a matter for concern – there is a need to account for the quality as well as the continuity of relationships with carers. For example, it seems plausible that 'mind-mindedness' could be protective, and be associated with attachment security, beyond infancy and beyond the parent–child relationship. Howe (2005) emphasizes its role in therapeutic and caregiving relationships with children and adolescents who have been maltreated, commenting that: 'Children need to let go of the fearful controlling behaviours that have actually served them well in environments of fear and danger, and instead begin to trust, value and enjoy open communication with a sensitive, mind-minded carer' (Howe 2005: 236).

In summary then, it appears that attachment theory highlights two key issues for children and young people in residential care. The first is the importance of the relationship between carer and child – providing an opportunity for the child to form an alternative internal working model of attachment that is secure, and promotes emotional security. The second, contingent, factor is what Meins terms 'mind-mindedness' – sensitivity to the child as an individual with a mind, rather than as a collection of needs, behaviours or risk factors.

Parental knowledge and monitoring

Since Baumrind (1967) offered her typology of parenting in terms of control (as permissive, authoritarian and authoritative), there has been much interest in both how parents understand and regulate their children's behaviour, and in disaggregating what might be called psychological and behavioural control (e.g., Barber 1996; Pettit et al. 2001; Smetana and Daddis 2002). Smetana and Daddis (2002: 523) define psychological control as 'parental attempts to control the child's activities in ways that negatively affect the child's psychological world and thereby undermine the child's psychological development', including intrusiveness, guilt induction and love withdrawal. Behavioural control can be understood as the rules and restrictions that parents have for the child, and their knowledge or awareness of the child's activities (often termed parental monitoring). This body of research indicates that high levels of psychological control, and inadequate behavioural control are frequently associated with behaviours defined as problematic (such as criminal offending or drug use). Further evidence suggests that parental knowledge of children's daily experiences is also an important factor – children whose parents know less about their day-to-day lives are more likely to show these sorts of problematic or risky behaviours (see Crouter and Head 2002 for a review).

Relative to the wider population, young people looked-after in residential care are at high risk of problems such as criminal offending or drug use. Would it therefore be informative to consider residential workers' caregiving in terms of theoretical models of parental control? One difficulty with that approach, in England at least, is that the rules and restrictions that provide 'behavioural control' for the child are stipulated in legislated regulations, although they are subject to interpretation and implementation by the child's carers. Similarly, requirements for documentation of young people's movements in and out of their establishments would appear at first glance to have addressed the issue of caregiver monitoring. That said, research increasingly indicates that parental knowledge is dependent on relationships with the child or young person, something that legislated procedures cannot address. Stattin and Kerr (2000) and Crouter and her colleagues (e.g., Crouter et al. 2005) have argued that parental knowledge entails more than monitoring or surveillance of child activities. It is, they suggest, a dyadic phenomenon, developing in the context of a trusting parent–child relationship, and dependent on the child's willingness to confide, rather than the parents' ability to track the child.

For example, Crouter and her colleagues (2005) found that parents defined as 'relational' knew significantly more about their teenage children's everyday lives than did other parents in the study, and, when interviewed by the research team, these young people reported fewer risky behaviours. 'Those with less positive relationships . . . may have to rely on others for information about their offspring, a style of knowledge acquisition that, our data suggest, is linked to lower levels of knowledge and, ultimately, higher levels of adolescent risky behaviour' (Crouter et al. 2005: 880).

In the context of residential care, it may be difficult to achieve this relational form of staff knowledge of young people's everyday lives. High staff numbers, relative to the number of young people looked after, could lead to reliance on others in the staff team for information, especially in an environment that has frequent turnover of young people and/or staff.

This discussion of parenting has highlighted the protective value of relationships, and of communication and attention to the child. As we will see in forthcoming chapters, pedagogy is sometimes conceived as upbringing, and as such its theoretical base draws on attachment theory and emphasizes the relationship between carer and child, as one person in relation to another. In England, as we shall also see, a minority of staff hold relevant qualifications for the work they do. Staff turnover is high (Mainey 2003) and English policy means that residential care is likely to be used as an interim measure or as a last resort, for children and young people whose needs and behaviours cannot be accommodated within foster care services. How, in this sometimes extreme and difficult context, is it possible to provide compensatory attachment models, through sensitive and responsive caregiving that (to paraphrase Meins et al. 2002) treats young people looked after as individuals with minds, rather than merely entities with needs that must be met?

The studies

At the time we undertook the research, the substantial disadvantage suffered by many looked-after children in England was very evident, and recognized by social policy (see Chapter 3). It was against this background that we set out to identify other options, tried and tested elsewhere, for conceptualizing and developing work with children in residential homes, and for the formation of the workforce involved in their care. The book draws on two connected studies conducted by the authors as part of an ongoing programme of work for the Department of Health/Department for Education and Skills.

Book contents

The two chapters in the first part of this book, pedagogy as education in the broadest sense, draw mainly on our first study, which used a qualitative approach to explore residential care policy and the part played by social pedagogy in five European countries: Belgium (Flanders), Denmark, France, Germany and the Netherlands. The study utilizes the reports of our European research associates and the interviews undertaken with civil servants, administrators, college and university lecturers and students, and staff in residential institutions. Chapter 2 begins with a discussion of what is meant by pedagogy and social pedagogy. The chapter describes in broad terms something of the work of the pedagogue, especially their use of themselves – skills, feelings, thoughts, and personhood – in relationship with the children whose everyday lives they share. The chapter is a necessary foundation for the more detailed and more quantitative findings presented in Part 2.

Chapter 3 presents further material from the first study, this time providing the context for social pedagogy: the different national policies towards residential care, the numbers of children in care and the proportions of these in residential care. We also provide some details on the training of residential staff in these countries. We outline some of the main differences in these matters between England and the other countries studied.

Part 2, Residential care in Denmark, England and Germany, consists of four chapters based on data drawn from our second study, a detailed comparison between residential care in Germany, Denmark and England. The second study used both quantitative and qualitative methods. Chapter 4 considers workforces issues, especially differences in training and levels of qualification in the three countries. It also considers staff commitment to their work and the related issues of the recruitment and retention of staff. Chapter 5 is about the different understandings and values that inform work in residential homes in the three countries, and about the content of the work. In Chapter 6, we examine how important aspects of children and young people's lives, such as schooling and contact with their families and with the local community relate to policy and practice. Chapter 7 is about the children themselves and how they report their relationship with staff and whom they can turn to when they need advice or support. As we shall see throughout this section, on many indicators, the English establishments did less well than those studied in Denmark and Germany. Nevertheless, some English establishments did better than others and the approach of staff was closer to that of the pedagogues in the other two countries. The section concludes with a presentation and discussion of three English residential establishments that appeared to be more supportive of children's development than others. The concluding section of the book considers the findings in terms of key messages for work with children that can be drawn from our examination of the pedagogic approach, including potential lessons for English policy and practice.

Details of the research designs and the methodology employed are provided in the Appendix.

PART 1

Pedagogy as education in the broadest sense

2   What are pedagogy and social pedagogy?

Introduction

Pedagogy and social pedagogy are terms that have aroused increasing interest in the UK over the last decade or so. In the UK and other English-speaking countries the word 'pedagogy' usually denotes the science of teaching and learning, and relates to the formal curriculum of school, college and university, what in continental Europe is sometimes referred to as 'didactics', rather than pedagogy. Across continental Europe, 'pedagogy' has a much wider meaning, the very breadth of which can at first be perplexing to a British ear. Much English language literature on social pedagogy comes from academics with an interest in social work and social work training (Davies Jones 1986; Cannan et al. 1992; Lorenz 1994; Crimmens 1998; Higham 2001) and, more specifically, in child care (e.g., Colton and Hellinckx 1993). A question often raised by this work is whether in some respects social pedagogy may be preferable to social work (although, as we discussed earlier, social pedagogy can be conceived of as a form of social work: social work within a reflexive-therapeutic framework).

In the UK, work with children is increasingly conceptualized as care work, but there are some suggestions of dissatisfaction with this term's adequacy or appropriateness. For example, 'children in care' became, with the Children Act 1989, 'looked-after children'. Yet, child care (note, two words) continues to be the policy field relating to looked-after children who are the responsibility of the local authority. Somewhat confusingly, childcare (one word) denotes a different policy field: namely those services for children whose parents work and need daily alternatives to parental care. In this field, descriptors such as 'educare', 'playcare' and 'early years services' seek to broaden the understanding of work with children, beyond the notions of responsibility and surveillance that often underpin 'care'. They provide a more educative perspective – while not limiting the work solely to the educational domain. An understanding that care and education are related is longstanding (Davies Jones 1986).

We first encountered the term pedagogy in earlier work conducted at the Thomas Coram Research Unit (for example, a survey of out-of-school services in the European Union (Meijvogel and Petrie 1996); work on children's services in Sweden (Moss and Petrie 2002); research into the changing role of the school (in integrating, for example, social work and health services) in Sweden, France and the USA (Moss et al. 1999). Nevertheless, until the work described in this book, we had not specifically addressed pedagogy itself. In the absence of closer scrutiny, pedagogues appeared to be out-of-school workers, classroom assistants, nursery teachers, care or social workers, occupations that appear, to English eyes to be somewhat disparate. While, for us, a full appreciation of the meaning of pedagogy developed quite slowly, it appears that we were not atypical in this respect: 'Despite decades of exchanges and collaboration it is still almost impossible to make English-speaking colleagues and students in social work understand the nature of social pedagogy' (Lorenz 1998: 26).

Importantly, the concept of pedagogy, as used outside the Anglophone world, relates to social work, childcare *and* education. A useful working definition of pedagogy is probably that of 'education in its broadest sense', or 'bringing up' children in a way that addresses the whole child. The necessity to indicate whether education is being used in a broad or a narrow sense leads to a central dilemma for English speakers. In the English language there is no single word that can stand for 'education in its broadest sense' to distinguish it from 'education associated with the academic curriculum'. But it is 'education in its broadest sense' that many continental Europeans mean when they talk about pedagogy.

In French, and some other Romance languages, *l'éducation* (or its cognates) is used to denote what in Northern Europe is known as pedagogy, while words such as *la scolarité* (schooling) and *l'enseignement* (teaching or instruction) are reserved for formal education. Crimmens (1998: 310), discussing the terms *l'éducation* and pedagogy, cites Tuggener (1986) who suggests that 'their commonality can be assumed owing to the similarities in the origins and historical development and the special forms of training which characterise contemporary practice across Europe'. In what follows, the term 'pedagogy' should be taken as covering the French term *l'éducation*, and allied terms in other Romance languages.

A further problem is that not only is 'pedagogy' used differently in the Anglophone world, but it is a term that can disappear in translation. In the papers that were translated for our studies, from French, Dutch, German, Danish and Flemish into English, 'pedagogy' was frequently mistranslated as 'education', and 'pedagogues' as teachers. At an international social work conference in Copenhagen in 2003, attended by members of the research team, speakers used English terms such as 'social care worker' to translate the descriptor 'social pedagogue' from their own language. Similarly confusing translations sometimes appear in the official English language brochures of colleges and universities in continental Europe. In translation of French documents, *l'éducation* may be mistranslated as 'education', *l'éducateur* becomes, equally misleadingly, a teacher and *l'éducation specialisée* is transformed into special education – when, in fact it is closer to English social work/social care.

We are faced therefore with the lack of an English term for pedagogy/ *l'éducation* because we have not yet fully developed this concept. The nearest UK equivalent to the pedagogue or *l'éducateur* is perhaps the use of 'social educator' to refer to youth workers – people who are interested in supporting young people's development, outside the formal education system.

Social pedagogy

A theory of social pedagogy (*Sozialpädagogik*) appears to have been first defined in 1844 by Karl Mager, as the 'theory of all the personal, social and moral education in a given society, including the description of what has happened in practice' (Winkler 1988: 41, as translated by Gabriel Thomas, the German associate for our first study). Broadly speaking, 'social pedagogy' is used to describe the work of services that are socially provided[1]. While the home is sometimes described as the first site for pedagogy, and parents as the first pedagogues, society also plays a part in providing pedagogic institutions, alongside or instead of parents. As a field, social pedagogy can accommodate provision such as childcare, youth work, family support, youth justice services, secure units, residential care and play work – services that, to British eyes, appear somewhat disparate. The use of the term 'pedagogy' allows for a discourse that can rise above differences based on, for example, the age of those who use services or a service's immediate goals; it permits any particular provision to be located in the context of a wider social policy towards children.

Core values of pedagogic training and practice

Although the pedagogic approach was well established in all the countries visited, interviewees nevertheless had some initial difficulty in answering the question, 'What is pedagogy?' It is not always easy to explain terms whose meanings are taken for granted by those who use them on a daily basis. (Explaining what English speakers mean by social work, or social care, to people without an insider perspective can be equally difficult.) Some of the people interviewed suggested that it is the very general nature of the field that makes definitions difficult. For example, the principal of the Copenhagen Social Pedagogic Seminarium commented that social pedagogy concerns 'everything', adding that it could be seen as an approach that underpins the training and education of pedagogues, rather than as a discrete area of study. This value-based interpretation was echoed by the principal of a training

college in France (Buc Resource) who observed that *L'éducation specialisée* '...
is an ideology – it is not a closed theoretical system'. Our analysis revealed a
consistency in pedagogic values and concepts across the countries we studied,
as an approach to work with children and young people.

What follows describes the main characteristics of the practice of pedagogy to emerge from the study.

Principles of the pedagogic approach

From one country to another, accounts of the characteristic approach of the
pedagogue revealed remarkably consistent principles:

- A focus on the child as a whole person, and support for the child's
  overall development;
- The practitioner seeing herself/himself as a person, in relationship
  with the child or young person;
- Children and staff are seen as inhabiting the same life space, not as
  existing in separate hierarchical domains;
- As professionals, pedagogues are encouraged constantly to reflect on
  their practice and to apply both theoretical understandings and self-
  knowledge to the sometimes challenging demands with which they
  are confronted;
- Pedagogues are also practical, so their training prepares them to share
  in many aspects of children's daily lives and activities;
- Children's associative life is seen as an important resource: workers
  should foster and make use of the group;
- Pedagogy builds on an understanding of children's rights that is not
  limited to procedural matters or legislated requirements;
- There is an emphasis on team work and on valuing the contribution
  of others in 'bringing up' children: other professionals, members of
  the local community and, especially, parents;
- The centrality of relationship and, allied to this, the importance of
  listening and communicating.

The work of the pedagogue emerged as essentially personal, with students,
college staff and residential staff speaking of the work of the pedagogue as
involving the whole human person: head, hands and heart.

A pedagogy of relationships – 'the heart'

> When you are holding a person in your hand, you are holding a bit of his life in your hand.
>
> (Principal of a Danish training college)

As we shall see in Chapter 3, in the countries that we studied, children are placed in residential homes more frequently than in England. The reasons for this go beyond a concern for child protection and safeguarding children. The intention that lies behind a care placement is often to provide a positive upbringing for children who do not receive this at home – or, in the case of short-term and weekday provision (where children go home at the weekend), to supplement what the parents can provide. The relationship between the child and the pedagogue is seen as the basis for a 'good' upbringing. A senior German civil servant said that it is 'pedagogic' to understand what child's needs are. There must be someone to whom the child can turn, who understands their needs and feels responsible for them. He believed that this sense of responsibility was the basis for the personal relationship between child and worker.

A Dutch professor of orthopedagogics (the theory of social pedagogy) referring to an ongoing discussion on the boundaries between subject areas and professions, said:

> Child psychiatry is more about deviant development, whereas child psychology is about normal child development. And pedagogical theory is specially about relationships, child-rearing relationships . . . the relationship a child has with [their] primary care giver, and mostly its parents, but also it could be a child care worker if they live in residential care.

The head of a children's residential establishment in Flanders said that each worker in the establishment had two or three children for whom they had a special responsibility. He defined this, not in administrative terms, but as:

> Being very interested in the child's wants, feelings, interests, thinking, fears and pleasures. On at least weekly basis they have an individual talk with the child. It is a more intimate relationship – because otherwise the child doesn't have any relationships, or deep contacts, they just have food and care. And that is institutionalising. You could say that staff have to be able to build close relationships with children. It is not trying to replace parental relationship – you have to pay close attention and respect that.

As part of our research, we asked pedagogy students to draw a 'good' pedagogue and a 'bad' pedagogue. This was intended to trigger discussion. A characteristic that featured in many drawings of a 'good' pedagogue, was the capacity of the worker to relate to children with warmth, symbolized as a heart, and spoken of as 'having room in your heart'.

Danish students and others referred to the term *rummelighed*, (meaning literally space or capacity), which derives from psychoanalysis and relates to notions of containment. This term implies the capacity to accept others, through self-knowledge, an awareness of one's own reactions and the dimensions of one's own personality which may resonate with those of the other person. In relationships, a person with self-knowledge is seen as being able to 'contain' another's feelings, their anger, sorrow or exuberance. To have *rummelighed* implies being able to work with difference and the capacity to involve the self in the other's life (Jensen 2001). It also underlies the need for warmth and compassion in pedagogic work. A Danish student said that a good pedagogue was one who had a 'professional heart'. While she did not have to like all the young people with whom she worked, she had to be prepared to use 'the self', that is her own humanity, to 'gain access to their way of thinking and feeling'.

In one children's home in Denmark, we were told that a night duty worker could be faced with several young people wanting to sleep on the floor of the small room used by staff who were sleeping over. In these circumstances, the worker could reserve the right to say 'enough is enough' and not accede to such requests. For these workers, recognizing children's needs was accompanied by an understanding of their own needs and a readiness to be open about them: dialogue and exchange of experience and perspectives is an important aspect of pedagogical work.

The responses of students and of residential staff to vignettes presented by the researchers also revealed physical contact with the child as an appropriate pedagogic practice (less thinkable in the UK after the scandals we referred to earlier). If a child was missing his or her parents, a worker in Denmark said she would, 'Take them in my arms, if I have good contact with them'. Another said she would, 'cuddle [him or] her, or she may make a bed up on the floor of the pedagogue sleepover room for the night' that is, the children could bring a mattress into the night staff's bedroom for the night. But she also recognized that 'some children cannot tolerate the physical intimacy involved in cuddling. You have to know the person and their limits of contact'.

A Dutch male student (B), who was working as a qualified nurse and doing a part time course (second year) said:

B: 'I guess it is a good start to hug her and hold her'
    [to which a second student (C) responded]

C: If you are a man, be careful.

B: Be careful, that's true!

C: You always have to be careful because most of the children have life problems and they can also tell them like 'he touched me'.

Listening – the ear

If pedagogy is based in human relationships, the quality of those relationships is linked to the quality of the interpersonal communication between children and staff. This is fostered through listening and dialogue. Listening to children's views was often stressed, both as a way of understanding their viewpoint and as a means by which children's wishes could be taken into account and acted upon. Accordingly, when we asked students to draw how they saw 'good' and 'bad' pedagogues, the pedagogue's ears were sometimes depicted. In line with the pedagogic principle that listening is the foundation of effective relationships, 'good' pedagogues were sometimes shown with big ears and 'bad' pedagogues with small ears, or no ears at all.

The following is a discussion between Dutch mature trainees (C and D) with a researcher (R) on one of their pictures of a bad pedagogue. It emphasizes the need to listen and relates this to team work, another key theme (see below):

C: He doesn't say much, but, and he also closes his eyes, you don't see ears. So I don't think he can see a lot and hear a lot ... He doesn't need expertise from other clients themselves. Yes, he has a solo position. He works in a solo position.

D: And I think it's very important for the social worker [the pedagogue] to work in a crew, not always alone.

R: Right. What's he saying? [Referring to a speech bubble]

D: He says, 'I can work on my own. I don't need opinions'.

C: Yes. Team work is very important. To listen to each other. But I think also for the ... I listen to the client. He has the central position. He is the expert who knows what he needs, I think.

Dialogue is seen as a critical tool in resolving the practical and emotional problems experienced by young people, everyday, with pedagogues routinely encouraging discussion and decision-making by groups and individuals. The head of a Flemish establishment said that some decades previously:

We managed with children while they were living here ... [i.e., they behaved 'well' during the time they were in residence] But as soon as they went home, you couldn't see anything [any outcome] from the experience of living in an institution – they returned to their old ways of living. That was a message for us – trying to keep up appearances does not work. For long-term outcome [it is] better to deal with discussion now, so they know [what to do] when they encounter a problem [they will] remember discussions they had in the institution.

He was proposing that to be effective, the discussion of any problems should include the children's points of view, not merely a statement of what staff believed. Pedagogues should have the ability to see the world as children saw it, if not what they had to say would have little relevance for children. Informants often spoke about listening in terms of respect for the children and of learning from them. At the same time the process of dialogue was seen as protective – part of a healthy upbringing.

A pedagogy of reflection – the head

It is precisely because social pedagogy places an emphasis on forming personal relationships with clients and colleagues that maintaining a proper balance between the personal and the professional is a key pedagogic skill. Here, the use of reflection is brought to bear. As with the heart, the head is also seen as having a role in pedagogy, and neither must dominate the other. Interviewees in all countries in the first study highlighted the need to 'preserve oneself' and to achieve a balance between appropriate closeness and sufficient distance to make judgements, since the emotional demands of the work could be high.

A French interviewee, the principal of a training college, said that *les éducateurs* (pedagogues) must be close to children, but not too close. They must know their roles and the limits of their roles – they are not equivalent to parents. And the head of a Flemish residential establishment for children with behavioural and emotional difficulties asked: 'Are personal relationships in a professional capacity difficult? Yes. Very – the main issue in team dynamics – how these relationships are [to be] kept professional. You have to keep boundaries if you want to make an evolution [i.e. if the child is to develop in a positive manner].'

Reflection on practice, in the light of theory and of the practical outcomes intended for young people, is seen as one means by which a proper balance may be achieved. In Flanders, we were told that one of the most important elements of pedagogic training was learning to work systematically, bearing in mind the goals identified for a young person, the background situation and the context in which the pedagogue works. It is only through reflection that all of these factors can be given proper weight. Staff and students of social pedagogy at the University of Lüneberg in Germany referred to the concept of *Haltung*, which literally means 'stance', but in this context indicates a professional stance and attitudes, combined with 'use of self' – a professional awareness of personal feelings, thought and experience as part of the pedagogue's resources.

Pedagogic reflection is implicit in the following account from a Dutch student. At the time of interview, she was doing an in-service training course part-time over four years, and was currently employed in a children's home. She said of her drawing of a 'good' pedagogue:

> When you look on his position he is stable and he has an open expression and he has big ears so he can hear a lot and also his eyes are wide open, but his mouth is not already open, because he first looks and hears . . . you have to look and hear very well . . . before you speak, before you can have your own words of [for] the situation. You have to make a good analysis of the situation of the client you are working with. The arms of the person are ready to do something, but first he has to look and hear and then he can handle [act] and before he handles [he must decide] how he has to speak.

Students in several countries discussed these issues in terms of trying to find a balance of head and heart. They suggested that working effectively as a pedagogue depends on 'acting spontaneously, but consciously', with spontaneous responses firmly grounded in professional training. While students drew hearts on the torsos of the good pedagogue to illustrate the importance of the giving of the self, of warmth and compassion, they also referred to the need not to become emotionally involved in the young people's lives. The broad range of pedagogic training was also seen as key in this respect; it was argued that the pedagogue must understand a broad range of issues and values, in order to develop a 'professional ethic'.

The principal of a French training college said:

> We train the directors [of residential establishments], the *éducateurs* and the monitors [staff working at a slightly lower level than the pedagogues]. Our philosophy is the same in training managers [directors] or *éducateurs*. They must understand economy, finance, regulation but also child development. The same values transcend all the professions we deal with here. They must also be able to make use of all sorts of theories. But students must [also] develop an open frame of mind.

Nordic pedagogues ally reflection on theory and practice to issues of accountability:

> The actions of the professional social educator (pedagogue) are a
> public matter and she must be able to explain to others the theory,
> i.e. what she wishes to achieve with her actions and the ethics on
> which the actions are based.
>
> (NFSS 2003: 13)

The notion of reflection is central to pedagogic training and practice. A
French pedagogue, working in a children's home, said, 'It is a job where every
day you must ask questions about yourself and your practice right to the end
of your professional life'. He went on to say that reflection must not only be at
an individual level, it should also be a regular function of the staff group. 'And
a well functioning team must discuss the work in order to do better. It is
appropriate for human beings – we are not machines.' In the Netherlands, a
student said of his drawing of a bad pedagogue, 'Doesn't want to be criticised.
Doesn't listen to it. Doesn't have a good reflection. Can't reflect on himself
and yes, the people who he is working with just have to do things and doesn't
want to discuss things with him. That's it.'

It was also apparent that the reflective practitioner drew others into the
process of reflection, and that one goal of pedagogy was to help children to
reflect on their own actions and on the consequences of various decisions.
The pedagogue who was not reflective would be a bad role model. The way in
which management behaved towards staff, and tutors towards students, was
referred to as presenting a pedagogic model. The head of a Belgian agency,
speaking of his relationship with staff said:

> This reflects the pedagogical way of working. We can't have one way
> for working with clients and another way of managing personnel.
> That is one of the points we think is a very important issue. If you
> expect your staff to have certain types of interactions with clients,
> you can't have different types of interactions with staff, [you] model
> how to behave. It is very pedagogic – take care of them but don't take
> responsibility away [from them]. Do the same with parents and
> children – it is your [way of] life.

The head of a French establishment echoed this, saying:

> You have to dress well to respect the children. For example, I wear a
> tie to show respect to staff and children. We have a good wooden
> table for our staff meetings [large polished board room table]. If you
> treat the staff well, they will treat the children well. All these things
> carry meanings. The children are very observant and notice every-
> thing.

An important process aimed for in pedagogic training is an awareness of the relationship between theory and practice and an ability to evaluate one against the other – and across the countries studied, the practice placement plays a large part in this. As one student interviewee said, 'A placement may be bad in that you made a lot of mistakes, but good in that you learned a lot'.

Two Danish authors write that to achieve a consciousness of learning, the student

> ...must gain awareness of the conditions under which her learning is best ... the acquisition of competencies towards taking a position as an active, reflective and responsible student ... how to be examining and reflecting, how to interpret and understand the surroundings and how to try to make this have a personal meaning and how to make choices and decisions.
>
> (Jensen and Christiansen 2000)

A central tenet of the pedagogic approaches studied was to reject universal solutions and accept a multiplicity of possible perspectives, depending on personal circumstances, particular dynamics, events and sources of support. For example, responses to many of the vignettes, that asked how workers would respond to children in various circumstances, emphasized that 'it depends', reflecting the preference for a critical professional judgement. Working in a pedagogic way is, therefore, not tied to technical procedures, but requires both an intuitive and a systematic synthesis of information, emotions and, critically, knowledge gained from study. Jensen, herself an educator of pedagogues (2000), notes that:

> Disciplines like psychology, philosophy, sociology and health science have major importance as theoretical support for social pedagogy, but in fact they rarely indicate the way to act in practical pedagogy. Rather, the worker uses these disciplines as a means of understanding why a young person acts as they do, and uses the knowledge in combination with continuous evaluation of 'the forms, relations and roles of coexistence in the relationship between the child and the adult, as well as everyday principles and rules'. It is usual to involve the users in these discussions ... The focus is on the client's personal story and his or her possibilities for development. The reflexive pedagogue must, by means of professional reflections, continuously reformulate and adjust the goals, means and actions encompassed in the pedagogical work.

The pursuance of such a reflective approach was seen in the 'multiverse' approach adopted by one of the Danish residential establishments visited.

Recognition of the child's 'multiverse' (as opposed to universe) requires that the staff do not try to impose one meaning on a situation, but think about the different meanings that differing perspectives and contexts might bring to a child's life and his or her difficulties – an understanding which is similar to the German pedagogic concept of the child's *Lebenswelt* or 'life world'. The concepts are used to encourage practitioners to seek children's perspectives, to understand the complex experiences from which these spring, and to accept the existence of a range of viewpoints. The concepts lead pedagogues to appreciate the significance of children's own families, and the importance for them of their peer groups and wider social networks.

A practical pedagogy – the hands

Alongside the contribution of the heart and the head, the third characteristic of pedagogy was practicality and engagement in activities with children and young people: 'the hands'. As a Flemish student said, 'You need to be out there and doing it, not just sitting around a table saying tell me what's your problem'.

The hands do not act in isolation from the heart and the head, but engage with them: relationships are realized through the medium of joint activities with children and provide a content and context for reflection. The principal of the French training college we visited described *l'éducation spe-cialisée* (specialized education or social pedagogy) as 'a way of being in the world, not just a way of thinking ... Professionals are people of action and know how to do something'. He saw life experience as a prerequisite for selection for training. This practical emphasis was echoed by interviewees in all the countries we visited and related to making and acting on decisions, looking after children and their physical and social needs, and engaging with children in domestic, creative and social activities.

Making and acting on decisions

For pedagogues, reflection and introspection must be balanced against the need for practical action – 'You must be able to mobilise yourself', said the French training college principal. He explained that in the course of their work, pedagogues had to think on their feet and take decisions quickly. These decisions would be informed by earlier reflections on practice, and would themselves be the substance for further reflection and evaluation, in a calmer moment.

In contrast – but not necessarily in contradiction – a Dutch part-time trainee said:

> But sometimes it is important not to take ... too much action ...
> Because I am working in a crisis centre for youngsters and most of the
> time they come in crisis, so for them it is very important to rest and
> to get, to feel good, to get out of the crisis. So for them it is very
> important not to do too much and not to ask too much from them.

Her remarks illustrate the key principle, frequently encountered in our
research, that action and decisions must depend on children's circumstances
and specific contexts.

Many examples of how pedagogues should act (and did so, customarily)
were given in the discussion of vignettes about situations involving young
people, which we presented to students and practitioners as trigger material
for discussion, and which our second study used in a more quantitative way.
Pedagogues' replies often showed that they would try to balance the needs of
all parties concerned, not forgetting the obligation to meet legal requirements.

For example, in discussing a vignette about children who did not wish to
attend school, while students and staff said that they would try to find out
what lay at the basis of the problem and would consult with school staff about
it. But the bottom line was that the law said that children had to go to school,
and that they would take the child to school. Two Dutch mature part-time
students, who were already working in the field, said as part of their discussion of this vignette, that they would comply with various legal frameworks
and institutional rules.

A: He has to go to school and until 16 he is forced to go to school.
B: But I also want to know why he does not want to go to school. What is
the real reason?

A French member of staff responded to the same vignette, 'The child has no
choice, it is obligatory ... I might say they could stay here and rest [if not well]
– but not watch TV. [I would] take their temperature. If they have no fever,
they must go to school'.

Similarly, a German worker's response to a vignette about children
smoking and drinking was, 'I have a responsibility to these children and
under 16 they are not allowed to drink or smoke. It's quite different if I do it
... I must tell them and insist on my responsibility [towards them]'.

Discussion of the vignettes revealed that staff and students felt, by and
large, secure in their duty to insist on a certain course of action when that was
supported by the law, or by the plan officially agreed for any particular child.

Looking after children

The practical nature of pedagogic work in residential establishments were often typified as domestic or parental duties, or as daily life together. A French pedagogue said of his daily routine:

> I wake them up, see that they make their beds, warm up the morning milk, just like mum. Take them to school. Come back and occupy my self with administrative work – the dossiers, phone the dentist, etc. At 11.30 I prepare the table for lunch. At one o'clock, take them back to school.

Many referred to helping with homework, making snacks with children, eating with them and watching television together. A German worker described her work as 'daily life' and listed the following activities which made up her days:

> Cooking and eating together, clearing and cleaning up together, making the place attractive together, going shopping with the young people, setting limits and talking about them, and providing a framework where they [limits] can be tested by individual young people, setting visiting times and times when children can go out, talking about these, helping with homework.

A Flemish head of establishment said that an applicant for a job in the establishment might have studied pedagogic theory at university, but that was a 'ticket to come and talk to us', and not a guarantee that the applicant would get a job. The person might have been a good student:

> But you have to be able to live it. To be able to live normal daily life but still able to be professional. From the outside, sometimes it looks as if he [member of staff] is doing nothing, he is just playing around with these children and giving them food. But he knows very well why he is laughing with this child, or giving this one some food. Always knowing why – and that's the difficult part. Learning and having studied allows you to make a framework of what is important.

Creative and practical skills

These comments put into perspective the requirement for pedagogy students to undertake courses in creative and practical activities. A special feature of pedagogic training in every country, at the level of first degree and below, were courses in sports and creative skills such as gardening, motor vehicle maintenance, music, art and theatre, often with the possibility to specialize in one of these. All of these could be put to use in everyday life in residential establishments, they were a medium in which relationships were formed. In England, a recent review of the role of the creative arts and play in promoting the well-being of looked-after children, concluded that,

> Creative arts and play can enhance the self-esteem and resilience of looked-after children, improve sensory awareness and help to counteract the consequences of childhood abuse and neglect. There is a place for carefully and supported arts and play workers in the looked after children's workforce
>
> (Chambers 2004: 1)

In addition, creative skills were seen as tools by which the pedagogue could work to build children's self-esteem. We often heard of the rejection that young people had experienced, in their families or at school. We were told that a primary aim of the pedagogic method was to address this history of rejection by identifying ways in which young people can experience success in small but achievable ways. Creative activities, with individuals and with the group, were seen as opportunities for children to achieve success and thereby raise their self-esteem. Creative activities could also be therapeutic in other ways. For example, in discussing a vignette where a worker hears a child crying during the night, some Dutch students suggested that the child could make a photo book of home, or make a collage.

Using the group

Many of the examples of practical and creative activities described above entailed the pedagogue sharing in the life of the whole group of children, whether in play, chores or creative activities. In addition, outdoor holidays taken as a group were a regular feature of residential care. These allowed group members to work closely and often to learn practical, sporting and creative skills together, drawing on the pedagogue's expertise. Practical activities could also be an opportunity to extend young people's knowledge and understanding of their society and to promote group discussion. The associative life of the group was seen as an important resource that workers should foster and make use of.

Workers and students, in discussing the problems posed by vignettes, often referred to making use of the whole group, perhaps in addition to an individual response. For example, in discussing how to address racist aggression, one method identified was that the staff group could take the theme of diversity as a basis for craft, outdoor activities and group discussions. This method was seen as encouraging young people to be more reflective about the issue than in the heat of a racist incident.

Staff in a German residential establishment remarked that all the young people in their home had experienced rejection by family, school or other children. It was, therefore, important that they became part of the group and did not feel rejected by it. This was achieved partly through the experience of daily life together, and partly through workers consciously drawing on their knowledge of group processes in order to strengthen relationships within the group.

Emancipation and respect

Our discussion of the part played by the head, hands and heart in the work of pedagogy, shows that the formation of pedagogues is not merely a matter of producing appropriate competences, it is also about fostering pedagogic attitudes; among these, as we have already shown, respect for the 'other' and their perspective, ranks high. In interviews and in documentation, we found that reference was often made to the UN Convention on the Rights of the Child, especially in Germany and Denmark. In Germany, students revealed that they were conscious that the child's right to express his or her wishes is enshrined in law (Child and Youth Welfare Act 1991), and that pedagogic work must respect that right.

We have also alluded to the tension implicit in helping young people to balance their own individual wishes with societal expectations, the tensions between processes of social control and processes of emancipation. This was a theme for other informants, also. Notes of an interview with the head of a Flemish establishment record:

> We have problems with many aspects of living together. To be correct with other people, be kind, have good manners and respect for other people, respect others' property. Living areas [the groups in which children live] are good training ... The aim for youngsters here is to develop in them the proper thinking – we don't want to think for them. It's a different approach to twenty to thirty years ago, when we tried to adapt children to society.

The difference between developing 'proper thinking' and 'adapting children for society' is a subtle one. However, it may perhaps be taken to mean educating children to act on the basis of principles, rather than reproducing set patterns of behaviour. Some interviewees held that work with children and young people should not direct or mould them, but enable them to use their rights and make decisions for themselves.

Flemish students raised the concept of emancipation in discussing the need to uphold the rules of an establishment while dealing with situations outlined in the vignettes we presented. They acknowledged the need for rules in a facility – 'At a moment of crisis you have to say no – for that second your word is law,' – but they generally agreed that rules can be ineffective, particularly if imposed on residents without discussion. They suggested that the staff and young people need to reach agreements that the young person understands. One student commented that, 'As adults we are always afraid to give authority to children, but it's not authority, it's responsibility'.

Discussion

In summary, this chapter has demonstrated something of the distinctive character of the social pedagogic approach: a focus on the whole child and support for the child's overall development and the engagement of the practitioner as a person, in relationship with the child, and bringing emotional, reflective and practical dimensions to the work. As discussed in Chapter 1, an approach that, in terms of parenting theory, conceives of children as beings possessed of minds and of distinctive perspectives, may well accrue the benefits of this approach, even though it finds its place in an institutional, rather than a family, setting. It would also appear that the pedagogic approach which we have identified works against institutionalization: it recognizes the person and their particular social life; it is not only reflective but also reflexive (a reflexive-therapeutic form of practice), with the practitioner in dialogue with young people, and their practice and understandings open to development as a result of that dialogue.

It is important to be aware, however, that the aims and values underlying pedagogy are culturally based: the aims of nineteenth century pedagogy differ from those of the twenty-first century. It would also be sensible to suppose that pedagogies such as those of a religious institution can be different from those of a secular institution, and that dominant political ideologies affect national pedagogies, and that the pedagogies developed within different welfare regimes are likely to have somewhat different emphases. We should not, therefore, think of pedagogy as having a fixed ethical and operational base. Lorenz asks:

> Is social pedagogy essentially the embodiment of dominant societal interests which regard all educational projects, schools, kindergartens or adult education, as a way of taking its values to all sections of the population and of exercising more effective social control; or is

> social pedagogy ... the thorn in the flesh of official agenda, an emancipatory programme for self-directed learning processes inside and outside the education system geared towards the transformation of society?
>
> (Lorenz 1994: 93)

As we have seen, some of the people we spoke to during the course of the research were aware of these debates, of the tensions that exist between pedagogy as an emancipatory process and pedagogy as a form of social control (the more individualist-reformist social work approach described by Payne 2005). These are tensions that are to be found in many of the 'social' occupations, including social work, social care and teaching. To us, it seems that the greater the commitment to 'the other' – the children and young people – as persons in their own right, to be listened to, and their interests respected, the more skilled the practitioners, the greater the likelihood of social pedagogy fulfilling more transformational ends. These were values much in evidence in the accounts of the people we interviewed.

Note

1   Social can also refer to the social or group dimension that is often seen as integral to pedagogy.

3 Looked-after children: national policies

Much of this book looks with a close focus at residential care, staffing, staff practice and the experience of young people. In this chapter, we describe some of the broader national policy contexts for residential care: the proportion of children in residential establishments, compared to foster care, together with an outline of training qualifications for residential work and how these two aspects of national policies may relate to each other. We also indicate, very briefly, how policy maps onto more theoretical concerns: the types of welfare regime represented and theories of social work and of parenting.

Table 3.1: Number of young people in residential care (data published at the time of study 1)

Country	Population (millions)	Young people in social care institutions	% of all looked-after children
UK	59.8	10371	14
Flanders	5.9	3086	53
Denmark	5.3	5907	54
France	60.2	52400	38
Germany	82.2	82051	59
Netherlands	16.3	9000	47

Sources:

UK: Combined figures for England, Wales, Scotland and Northern Ireland; Children looked after by local authorities, year ending 31 March 2001: Regional Trends 37, National Statistics (2001) (see http://www.statistics.gov.uk/STATBASE/ssdataset.asp?vlnk=5950)

Flanders: Figures provided by the Bureau for Special Youth Assistance, Ministry of the Flemish Community (personal communication, 2001).

Denmark: Assistance for Children and Young People (1998), cited in Jensen (personal communication, 2001).

France: DREES Etudats et Résultats, Ministère de l'Emploi et de la Solidarité, November 2002

Germany: Federal Statistical Office: Fachserie 13, Reihe 6.1.2, Reihe 6.1.4: Jugendhilfe – Erzieherische Hilfen außerhalb des Elternhauses, (1998) (see http://www.akj-stat.fb12.uni-dortmund.de/)

Netherlands: Figures provided by van der Ploeg and Scholte (personal communication, 2001). Population data from January 2004, source: http://statline.cbs.nl/StatWeb/Start.asp?lp=Search/Search&LA=EN&DM=SLEN

Numbers of children in care

The data presented in Table 3.1 indicate that a much smaller proportion of young people in the UK are looked after in residential institutions relative to the other countries. This variation can be explained in part by the way in which statistics are formulated. For example, in Germany young people often continue to use residential services until well into their twenties (usually in the form of quasi-independent living facilities), and these young adults appear in statistics on looked-after young people. Nevertheless the difference between the UK and other countries is striking. Variation in statistics, particularly in the proportion of young people looked after in residential units, also reflect a difference in attitude to institutional provision, which may in turn be related to the role of pedagogy in policies for looked-after children. As we have indicated in the last chapter, residential units in countries we visited in the first phase of the research were conceived by interviewees as positive sites for children's upbringing and development, without the connotations that 'institutional care' has to British ears.

Pedagogic ideas were clearly in evidence in policies for residential care provision in the countries studied. German, French and Flemish legislative documents explicitly state that their policy is pedagogic, and guidelines for residential facilities in Flanders and Denmark specify that children and young people should be cared for in a pedagogic way. Various French policy documents place looked-after children in an explicitly 'educative' framework. This holds good across various French government ministries for the example, whether children are the responsibility of youth justice or of social assistance. We should note, again, that when the term 'educative' is used, this does not denote schooling or formal education, but relates to education in the widest sense of that word.

Fostering made a substantial contribution to child care in each of the countries studied, but except for the Netherlands, was less common than placements in residential establishments. The number of children in Germany who were in residential care rose by 18,000 (27 percent) between 1990 and 1999. In the UK, there has been a deliberate and sustained policy preference for fostering, which has several causes including problems with the quality of care provided in large institutions, the high cost of keeping children in these establishments and recent scandals about child abuse that we outlined earlier. Importantly, foster care is generally seen as approximating more closely to a 'normal' upbringing than is possible in an institutional placement. It may also make for greater social integration within the local community and, perhaps, be less stigmatizing. However, the supply of foster homes does not meet demand in any of the countries studied and an appropriate foster home may not be available to meet emergencies. Furthermore, some young people are more difficult to place in foster homes than others; they include older children, sibling groups, children who are members of minority ethnic groups and children presenting challenging behaviour (Utting 1991; Waterhouse 1997). It seems likely that residential institutions will continue to play an important part in provision for looked-after children in all of the countries studied.

Qualification for work in residential settings

Deliberate efforts to professionalize the residential care workforce – through pedagogic training – were set out in legislation in all the countries we visited, and implemented, so that the proportion of trained staff working in residential settings was significantly greater than that to be found in the UK (we look at qualification levels, comparing Denmark, Germany and England, in Chapter 4). In England, minimum standards specified that from 2005, at least 80 percent of care staff should have a Level Three NVQ in Caring for Children and Young People, a lower level of qualification than those required in the other countries studied. But, despite public investment, completion rates look unlikely to meet this target (Mainey 2003). In the Netherlands, 91 percent of staff in residential facilities were qualified and French state-run facilities required a ratio of one qualified *éducateur spécialisé* for every five or six young people. A German civil servant commented that staff training had economic benefits for the local authority: 'Everyone should have it [the pedagogy degree] in order to have the appropriate skills. This will save us money in the end because they will work well with the children and maybe they can return home earlier'.

A brief overview (summarized in Table 3.2) of the training programmes available in each country follows. As the table indicates, undertaking a pedagogic qualification, even at a lower level, requires a substantial commitment of time; in general, however, the main qualification to be a pedagogue takes around three to four years. Courses provide students with a broad theoretical base for their work, drawing on academic disciplines such as psychology, sociology and criminology, and relevant theories, for example, attachment theory, group dynamics and labelling theory. More practical professional skills and knowledge are also covered: working with groups, the law relevant to children, conflict management and so on. It is also recognized that, because in many settings pedagogues spend their days living with the children, creative and practical everyday skills are a necessary part of their work; the students undertake, therefore, one or more activities such as sport, art, music-making, drama, car mechanics or gardening. In addition, practice placements are an ongoing part of the course. In many colleges, students undertake practice placements in other countries.

Table 3.2: The main pedagogical qualifications and educations in Belgium (Flanders), Denmark, France, Germany and the Netherlands

	Flanders	Denmark	France	Germany	the Netherlands
Vocational diploma:	*Hogeschool:* Graduate diploma in orthopedagogy.	*Pedagogic Seminarium:* Ordinary diploma in pedagogy.	*École Diplôme:* Éducation spécialisé.***	*Fachhochschule:* Diploma in social pedagogy.	*Fachschule Erzieher:** Diploma in social pedagogy.	*Hogeschool:* Diploma in social pedagogic support.
Duration:	3 years	3.5 years	3 years	4 years	3 years	4 years
Course content:	Broad theoretical base, practical training, sport and creative skills.	Broad theoretical base, practical training, sport and creative skills.	Broad theoretical base professional and creative skills.	Broad theoretical base, practical training, sport and creative skills.	Broad theoretical base, practical training, sport and creative skills.	Broad theoretical base, practical training, sport and arts.
Practice placement:	3 weeks in Year 1; 8 weeks in Year 2; 17 weeks in Year 3.	3 months in Year 1; 6 months in Year 2; 6 months in Year 3.	One of 1 month; two of 2 months; one of 7–9 months.	2 days/week: semester 4; 6 months: semester 5; 2 days/week: semester 6.	Two of 6 months.	0.5 days/week in year 1; 1 day/week in year 2; 10 months in year 3.
Other qualification:	*University Licenciaat* in Orthopedagogy.**	More theoretical university diplomas and higher degrees.	Various university degrees in *Sciences de l'éducation.*	*University diploma* in Social pedagogy.	*University diploma* in Social pedagogy.	*University Doctoraal* in Pedagogic Science
Duration:	5 years	4 years or more	4–8 years or more	4 years	4 years	
Course content:	Eclectic, mainly theoretical.	Theoretical and depending on specialisms.	Mainly theoretical.	Mainly theoretical, with management and administration.	Eclectic, mainly theoretical.	

*Notes: * The term *Erzieher* derives from *Erziehung*, which literally translates as bringing up or pulling up. ** Equivalent to Masters level qualification in the UK. ***In France there is also the *École Certificat* as *Éducateur Moniteur* is a lower level training, not a full qualification, taken over 2 years.*

In all the countries studied, there are also more theoretical pedagogic degrees, including higher degrees. These do not always serve as a qualification for employment as a pedagogue, but are seen, rather, as a preparation for administration or research in the sector relating to children and young people.

Belgium (Flanders)

The concept of pedagogy is highly evolved in Flanders, and distinctions are made between different forms of pedagogy, and in levels of training. For example, *Orthopedagogy* is the specialization that focuses on children and young people in special circumstance such as children in care, work with disabled people and work connected with youth justice. In interviews with course tutors, we were told that orthopedagogics is the most popular degree within the Faculty of Pedagogic Sciences at Ghent University. Employment rates among *licenciaat* graduates are high, with most going on to work in managerial roles as coordinators of teams and services. Within the field of orthopedagogics, we were told that, 'Students go on to work with all sorts of client groups ... This is the advantage of the broad education' (Professor of Orthopedagogics, University of Ghent).

Denmark

Training to be a pedagogue in Denmark is centrally regulated, professionalized and well-resourced. Pedagogic training is one of the most popular professional training courses in Denmark, described as more popular than teaching or medicine. The ordinary diploma in pedagogy, at degree level, is undertaken in special training colleges. It takes three and a half years and qualifies the student for work in a wide variety of settings. The pedagogy diploma is the 'usual' qualification for work with children in nurseries and preschools, school age childcare and residential homes. It is also a qualification for working with adults in, for example, mental health and other settings where adults need additional support. As in the other countries studied, pedagogy courses can be undertaken on a part-time basis. In addition, more theoretically based university courses are available.

France

France has three forms of *éducateurs*, relevant to work with looked-after children. *Les éducateurs specialisés* are trained to work with children, adolescents and adults experiencing difficulties arising from disability or because of

problems encountered in their family or personal life. This is the main profession for work with children and young people in residential care, with a
special role in the support of children in foster care. Students train for three
years, full-time, or 4–5 years in-service training, post-*baccalauréat* (school
leaving examination). They must be at least 23 years old, and have three or
more years of relevant work experience. Other *éducateurs* are trained for four
years, to work with children in the youth justice system. *Les éducateurs de
jeunes enfants*, are employed to work with children aged 0–7, in settings from
residential care to day nurseries. Training, at a lower level (that of *l'éducateur
moniteur*), follows a similar framework to the diploma in specialized education, but is a two year course. There are also theoretical university degrees that
prepare students for administration and research.

Germany

Training for work with children in Germany takes place in institutions of
both further and higher education. There are three distinct levels of training.
The most basic of these is a three year vocational college (*Fachschule*) qualification as a state approved *Erzieher* ('upbringer'). Universities of applied sciences (*Fachhochschule*) offer a four year degree in social pedagogy, the
preferred form of qualification for employment within children and youth
services, including residential care. Universities also offer degrees and higher
degrees in social pedagogy, although – as in other countries – university
qualifications usually lead to managerial or supervisory positions, rather than
work in residential care.

The Netherlands

Dutch training and practice distinguish between a variety of forms of pedagogy. Orthopedagogy refers to work with children who have developmental
problems or disabilities, while *sociaal pedagogische hulpverlening* (social pedagogic help-giving) takes four years full-time and is the most usual qualification for residential care work. There are also lower level courses for school
leavers, including a three year qualification in social pedagogic work (*sociaal-
pedagogisch werk*). Social pedagogic workers can be employed to work with
children and young people in residential care, but the majority (95 percent)
go on to higher education. There are also more theoretical university degrees.

Qualification and social policy

The approach to the education and training of pedagogues is not identical in the countries studied. There are somewhat different models in different parts of continental Europe, which may relate to different forms of welfare regime (see Chapter 1).

Denmark, representing the Nordic socialist democratic welfare model, requires a large, trained and educated workforce, mainly for employment in state provided, wide-spread universal services (such as nurseries and free-time/out-of-school services), but also for special welfare settings. It is in Denmark that we find a universal model of initial training and qualification, that of the pedagogue, for work across settings – although this is not necessarily the model adopted in other Scandinavian countries.

In what Esping-Anderson (1999) describes as the continental European or conservative welfare states (covering Belgium, France, Germany and the Netherlands), the emphasis for social pedagogy is on preparation for work with disadvantaged groups, but (i) for work across a range of community and special settings and (ii) sometimes with the qualification recognized for work in mainstream services (for example, for work in out-of-school services in Germany, where only 8 per cent of staff in such services are unqualified, while most of the rest have three to five years of training). It is in these countries, also, that we find more differentiated pedagogical trainings and qualifications for different settings.

Nevertheless, the research found common threads that run through training for social pedagogy in the countries studied. Other work (e.g., Courtioux et al. 1986) suggests that these commonalities hold throughout the continental European tradition. Preparation for pedagogical work – whether alongside parents or, at least partially, replacing parents – has much in common in all five countries. These commonalities include exposure to a range of theoretical and therapeutic frameworks, training in the methods and skills necessary for work with individuals and groups, the development of the student's creative and/or practical competence, practice placements and, often, international experience. In addition, the universities furnish a more academic and education, and develop pedagogic theory, to inform practice, policy and training. There is a thorough-going and coherent system of training and education for people working with children – including looked-after children. This means that practitioners and many of those employed in policy development and administration can operate within the same knowledge framework. It may be that the existence of a more common mind across the fields of policy and practice, together with the high level of qualification required and provided for residential care, all make for a greater trust in residential establishments than is to be found in UK policy.

The UK, which can be situated within the Anglo-Saxon, neo-liberal model of welfare has not developed in the same way as have the continental countries which we studied. In the UK's main universal services for children (education and health) most staff working directly with children are qualified to degree level. But it is only recently that public policy has turned towards the development of an educated and professional workforce for more specialized services, such as residential care. In addition, lacking the concept of pedagogy as 'education in the broadest sense', residential work, in the UK, has been conceptualized as 'care work' or 'social work' – neither of which concepts have the power of pedagogy to focus on the child as a minded, developing human person – in the ways that research that we described earlier (Chapter 1) has attributed to the 'good' parent. This is not to say that social work and care do not offer their own ethical and practical traditions for work with children. However we would suggest that a stream of pedagogic social work, situated in the reflexive therapeutic theory of social work, needs to be developed, if residential care is to become a more trusted, and more child focused, form of provision in Britain. We return to these ideas in later chapters and in our conclusions.

PART 2
Residential care in Denmark, England and Germany

4 Workforce issues in residential care

Introduction

In the preceding section of this book, we have described in general terms aspects of social pedagogy and children's residential care in five countries in continental Europe. Building on this background, in this section we focus more closely on policy and practice in three countries: England, Denmark and Germany, and research conducted in 49 establishments in these countries. This chapter examines the characteristics of staff, drawing on accounts given by 56 heads of residential establishments or units, and by 144 staff (see Table 4.1).[1]

Table 4.1: Number of heads of establishment and staff interviewed

	England N	Germany N	Denmark N	Total N
Establishments:	25	12 ⎫	12	49
Heads:	25	19 ⎬ *	12	56
Staff:	54	51 ⎭	39	144

Note: * In German institutions with more than one living unit on site, the heads of living units were interviewed in addition to the manager of the whole institution.

Chapter 5 compares the approaches of pedagogues and care workers to their work with children, while Chapters 6 and 7 focus on children's use of services, including their school attendance and their experience in residential care.

The data presented in this chapter are based on interviews and questionnaires (the design and methods are described in detail in the Appendix at the end of this volume). Cross-country differences were investigated statistically using analysis of variance and cross-tabulation, as appropriate. A qualitative analysis was utilized for the verbatim responses of staff and children to open-ended interview questions.

In this chapter we discuss, in turn, the attributes, skills and knowledge that residential care workers bring to their work, some aspects intrinsic to workers' experience of employment, such as their commitment and sense of satisfaction, and some aspects of the work that are more extrinsic to the experience of employment, such as the recruitment and retention of staff.

The chapter is divided into two parts. First, some broad characteristics of residential workers will be discussed, drawing on published national statistics, as well as findings derived from questions asked of heads of residential establishments included in the study. This first part will also include a discussion of the training and career development of residential workers. The second part will discuss recruitment and retention issues, drawing on the marked differences in the reports of heads of establishments in England, as compared with those in Denmark and Germany. Overall, we will show that while some workforce characteristics are similar across countries, others, such as the level of education for the work, and the extent of difficulty in recruiting staff, differ markedly.

Staff characteristics

Three important characteristics of the residential staff we interviewed did not show statistically significant differences across the three countries: gender, age and ethnicity. Most of the workers were female (ranging from 53 percent in Denmark to 66 percent in England and 76 percent in Germany, a trend which did not reach statistical significance). This gender imbalance was less pronounced than has been found in other forms of care work in England (Simon et al. 2003). The average age of residential staff in the present study was 39, and the proportion of ethnically white workers varied from 73 percent in England to over 90 percent in Germany and Denmark.

As we described briefly in Chapter 3, the extent to which workers hold relevant qualifications for residential care, and the level at which those qualifications are pitched, differs significantly across the three countries. In order to compare qualification levels across countries, it is necessary to understand what is available and expected in each country and to create comparable levels of qualification. Using the SEDOC levels[2], the common frame of reference for training, adopted by the European Community in 1985 (Van Ewijk et al. 2002), we have defined specific childcare qualifications in terms of high, medium and low.

In Denmark, as we saw in the last chapter, pedagogues achieve degree level qualifications, fitting them for work in a range of settings. We define this as a 'high level' qualification.

In Germany, on the other hand, there are three forms of pedagogic qualification: (i) a 'medium' level qualification to become an *Erzieher* (an 'upbringer'), taking three to four years; (ii) a degree-level qualification in social pedagogy – a 'high' level of qualification and the preferred qualification among German residential care employers – and (iii) a further 'high' level qualification: a more theoretical university degree in social pedagogy.

In England, the main qualification for residential care work is the competency award NVQ (National Vocational Qualification) Level 3 in Caring for Young People. Level 3 is designed to be equivalent to an Advanced Level General Certificate of Secondary Education (which itself is usually obtained at around the age of 18 years). The NVQ Level 3 is seen as appropriate for those working without supervision (QCA 1999). The award is usually workplace-based and takes about 18 months to complete, although as the learning progresses at the students' and assessors pace, this can vary widely (Cameron et al. 2003). For the purposes of cross-national comparison, we define this as a 'medium' level qualification, with NVQs below level 3 defined as 'low level'.

Table 4.2: Highest qualification for residential care, reported by staff by country (numbers and percentages)

Qualification	England N (%)	Germany N (%)	Denmark N (%)	Total N (%)
Low:	4 (8)	0 (0)	0 (0)	4 (3)
Medium:	18 (36)	22 (45)	1 (3)	41 (31)
High:	10 (20)	25 (51)	30 (94)	65 (50)
Other childcare qualification:	0 (0)	1 (2)	0 (0)	1 (1)
None/no relevant qualification:	18 (36)	1 (2)	1 (3)	20 (15)
Total:	50 (100)	49 (100)	32 (100)	131 (100)
Missing cases:	4 (–)	2 (–)	7 (–)	13 (–)

Table 4.2 sets out the highest qualification reported by the staff inter-viewed. Nearly all the pedagogues in Denmark held a high level relevant qualification (including, predominantly, pedagogy, but also social work and psychology), compared with half of those in Germany and one-fifth of those in England. Around one-third of the English workers held a medium level qualification, including the NVQ Level 3, and a further third held either no qualification or none that was relevant to their post. These figures are broadly comparable with those found in other English studies (McQuail 2001; TOPSS 2003; Brannen et al. forthcoming). Residential care workers in Germany were almost equally divided between medium and high level qualifications.

Heads of establishments

Fifty-six heads of establishment took part in the study, 57 percent of whom were male and 43 percent female. A higher proportion of establishment managers were male in Germany (75 percent) than in England (48 percent) and Denmark (58 percent). Data were not collected on the age or ethnicity of heads of establishments.

Table 4.3: Professional backgrounds of heads of establishment by country, numbers and percentages

	England N (%)	Germany N (%)	Denmark N (%)	Total N (%)
Pedagogy:	1 (4)	8 (67)	6 (50)	15 (31)
Social work:	20 (80)	3 (25)	1 (8)	24 (49)
Teaching:	2 (8)	0 (0)	2 (17)	4 (8)
Other:	11 (44)	6 (50)	7 (58)	24 (49)
Total:	25 (100)	12 (100)	12 (100)	49 (100)
Missing:	0 (–)	7 (–)	0 (–)	7 (–)

Note: A multiple response table: heads could have more than one response. Therefore columns may not sum to 100%

Table 4.3 sets out the professional backgrounds of heads of establishments: these varied both within and between countries. In Danish public sector homes, heads often reported having a background in psychology as well as pedagogy. In England, national occupational standards stipulate the skills and knowledge expected of managers (TOPSS 1999, 2003) stating that they should be 'appropriately qualified with appropriate levels and mix of care and managerial competences' (TOPSS 1999). In Germany, the main qualification for heads of establishments is the Diploma in Social Pedagogy from either a university or a *Fachhochschule* (70 percent of managers in one region held this qualification in 1999 (McQuail 2001). Overall, heads of establishments were highly experienced. On average, they had been in their current post for ten years, ranging from 19 years in Denmark to six years in England.

Continuous professional development and job satisfaction

Ongoing training was regarded as important for residential care workers across the three countries. In England, responsibility for the ongoing training of staff was at the time of writing embedded in national occupational standards for managers in residential child care (TOPSS 2003). These standards stipulate an induction process for new recruits, and ongoing training through NVQs, short courses and in-house training. These courses are intended to extend the knowledge and skills of staff in particular areas of work, and to ensure that residential institutions meet regulatory standards. Typically, such short courses are of one or two days' duration.

It might be hypothesized that a country with a low level of qualification for its residential care staff would have a high level of ongoing training in order to compensate for this deficiency. Accordingly, English staff should have a higher level of ongoing training than those in the other two countries. However, nearly all heads of establishment in all three countries reported that they themselves had had ongoing training (England, 95 percent; Germany, 92 percent; Denmark, 83 percent – differences not statistically significant). Virtually all the residential staff across the three countries had also received some kind of training, only three reported no training at all (Table 4.4).

Table 4.4:   Training received by staff interviewed, by country, numbers and percentages

Relevant training received	England N (%)	Germany N (%)	Denmark N (%)	Total N (%)
No training received:†	2 (4)	1 (2)	0 (0)	3 (2)
In-house training:*	27 (54)	38 (76)	30 (79)	95 (69)
Other short course:*	36 (72)	22 (44)	22 (58)	80 (58)
Training leading to some relevant qualification:**	26 (52)	40 (80)	37 (97)	103 (75)
Other:**	5 (10)	5 (10)	18 (47)	28 (20)
Total number of staff:	50 (100)	50 (100)	38 (100)	138
Missing cases:	4 (–)	1 (–)	1 (–)	6

Notes: † Not significant; * p<0.05; ** p<0.001. A multiple response table: staff could have received more than one type of training. Therefore columns may not sum to 100%.

In Germany and Denmark, staff were more likely to have received in-house training than in England, where residential care workers were more likely to report undertaking 'other short courses', often oriented towards regulatory and other requirements for residential homes.

Asked to list their courses, many informants in England recalled they had undertaken a wide range of short courses such as: preparing young people for independent living, first aid, essential health and safety, food hygiene, fire safety, mental health, child protection, anti-discriminatory practice, restraint with care, the Children Act, HIV/AIDS, drugs and alcohol awareness, moving furniture and other heavy weights, report writing, fire training and attachment theory. Further mentions were made of courses on working with autistic children, male rape, anger management, managing conflict, sexual health and relationships, working with groups and individuals, differences in the staff team and making daily risk assessments. Staff with a management role reported having taken courses in disciplinary training, action planning, best practice seminars, employment review, supervision, staff development and appraisal.

The range of courses listed suggests that in-house and short course training in English residential care homes serves both to meet regulatory requirements and to extend the knowledge and skills of residential care workers, who might well be starting from a very low specialist knowledge base (see Table 4.2). It might be argued, also, that many of the courses listed had an 'instrumental' orientation: that is, they were designed to meet the needs of the occupation and the institution, rather than to provide each worker with a broader education.

In Denmark, where nearly all the staff interviewed held a high level qualification, mostly in pedagogy, ongoing training was seen as an opportunity for further specialization. The degree in pedagogy was seen as 'basic' training for the work. Informants in Denmark, who had completed ongoing training had often done so away from work, in some cases for a year. Their training had been aimed at extending the range of skills, managerial or therapeutic, they had already acquired. For example, courses listed by pedagogues included a one year course in milieu therapy, two years' systemic education and family therapy, a one year study of pedagogy and organizations, one year's systemic interventions and family consultant courses. Training in Denmark could often be typified as therapeutic training, in that most of the courses reported were about improving the types, depth and level of interventions, available for repairing 'damage' among young people in their care.

German residential care workers usually held a pedagogic qualification, either at the high or medium level. Their ongoing training courses consisted mostly of short courses in relevant theory, and/or academic study, such as psychology and systemic therapy, group dynamics, juvenile justice, as well as practical training for writing reports and so on. These courses were aimed at improving academic knowledge and extending professional skills, and could be typified as 'professional' in character.

Perspectives on training

Perspectives on positive and negative aspects of training are best located within specific learning cultures, which vary across the three countries which we studied. This became apparent when staff were asked to discuss positive and negative aspects of training, whether initial or ongoing. Table 4.5 sets out cross-country differences in the many positive aspects of training reported by staff, in answer to the question: 'Thinking about any relevant training you have received, what would you say were the most positive aspects of that training for your work here with children and young people?'

Overall, answers to this question revealed a high level of commitment to training. Training afforded opportunities for personal and professional development, and for discussing work with others. It could contribute to 'a practitioner reflective environment' (the answer of one English worker) and could thus improve teamwork. Allied to this developmental aspect was the opportunity to 'replenish the spirit' and recuperate energy through having a day away from the workplace. Training was appreciated because it allowed staff access to both theoretical and practical knowledge. A few workers referred to practice placements, with an opportunity to combine theoretical and practice learning, as very useful.

Table 4.5: Positive aspects of relevant training received by staff for their work with children and young people by country, numbers and percentages

Positive aspects of training	England N (%)	Germany N (%)	Denmark N (%)	Total N (%)
Working with children's problems:***	18 (40)	1 (2)	15 (39)	34 (26)
Preparation for working directly with young people:***	16 (34)	6 (12)	0 (0)	22 (17)
Professional confidence:***	8 (17)	8 (17)	20 (53)	36 (27)
Knowledge of legal framework:†	5 (11)	11 (22)	2 (5)	18 (14)
Working with other staff within the establishment:*	4 (8)	0 (0)	5 (13)	9 (7)
Relationships with the children:***	3 (6)	0 (0)	12 (32)	15 (11)
Knowledge of methodology (techniques for practice):***	3 (6)	24 (50)	8 (21)	35 (26)
Working with families:***	2 (4)	1 (2)	9 (24)	12 (9)
Dealing with external agencies:†	2 (4)	2 (4)	2 (5)	6 (5)
Self-orientated (e.g., gaining qualification, career development):†	1 (2)	4 (8)	1 (3)	6 (5)
Theoretical knowledge of social pedagogy:***	1 (2)	16 (33)	5 (13)	22 (17)
Management training:†	1 (2)	0 (0)	3 (8)	4 (3)
Contacts with other students:†	1 (2)	5 (10)	5 (13)	11 (8)
Knowledge about other social sciences:***	0 (0)	16 (33)	3 (8)	19 (14)
Practice placements:**	0 (0)	12 (25)	8 (21)	20 (15)
Encourages critical/reflective practice/ analysis:***	0 (0)	2 (4)	9 (24)	11 (8)
Teaches new practical or creative skills:†	0 (0)	3 (6)	0 (0)	3 (2)
Inspires or renews motivation:*	0 (0)	0 (0)	3 (8)	3 (2)
All training useful or satisfying:†	4 (8)	4 (8)	3 (8)	11 (8)
Theory and practice combined helped:†	0 (0)	2 (4)	1 (3)	3 (2)
Other:†	2 (4)	2 (4)	5 (13)	9 (7)
No positive aspects mentioned:†	2 (4)	3 (6)	1 (3)	6 (5)
Total number of staff:	47 (100)	48 (100)	38 (100)	133 (100)
Missing cases:	7 (–)	3 (–)	1 (–)	11 (–)

Notes: † Not significant; * p<0.05; ** p<0.01; *** p<0.001. A multiple response table: staff could have mentioned more than one positive aspect of training. Therefore columns may not sum to 100%.

Staff in England reported most commonly that training helped them to work with children's and young people's problems (40 percent), and was a preparation for working directly with young people (34 percent). They also mentioned that training increased professional confidence (17 percent). Qualitative analysis of staff responses suggested that those in English establishments tended to report training in an instrumental way, in terms of being taught, as one informant said, to, 'Do things in the right way, giving you a grounding so things can't go wrong'. Some reported that they had gained in confidence, had better communication skills and could better reflect upon practice. Compared with staff in the other two countries, rather few of the staff in England reported other benefits accruing from training.

In Germany, staff spoke much less about working directly with children and their problems. They were more likely to cite the acquisition of knowledge such as pedagogic methods (mentioned by 50 percent), social pedagogy theory (33 percent) and other social sciences (33 percent) as benefits of training. They referred to the importance of practical training, for example, in arts and crafts, free time activities, sport, writing reports, file-keeping.

The staff in Denmark, on the other hand, most frequently spoke in terms of training increasing professional confidence (53 percent). They also thought that training was helpful in working with children's problems (39 percent). Unlike the staff in England, none of them identified preparation for working directly with young people, as a benefit of training. They were, after all, already highly qualified. They also identified a range of other benefits including those concerning relationships with children (32 percent), working with families (24 percent), reflective practice (24 percent) and techniques for practice (21 percent). A pedagogue in Denmark referred to being able to refine their own perspective on human development (*Menschenbild*) through reflective training opportunities that sometimes involved all members of staff in their establishment. In Danish establishments, informants tended to discuss training in terms of giving their work new dimensions, such as 'more depth, understanding and maturity'.

Less positive aspects of training

Fewer staff reported negative rather than positive aspects of training. Fifty-eight percent of staff in Denmark, 29 percent in England and 18 percent in Germany made no adverse comments about training (p<0.001).

Where staff did express adverse opinions, these were often very specific and localized, relating to a particular course undertaken in the past. There were also three general complaints about training. First, the balance between theory and practice present in training courses was criticized by some staff, sometimes in favour of theory and sometimes in favour of practice. Some of the workers in England said the NVQ was too theoretical, that more specialist training should be aimed specifically at residential workers and at experienced workers. In Denmark, some pedagogues said their training was insufficiently theoretical and was not pitched high enough 'to avoid boredom'. In Germany, a worker said that a correct balance between practical and theoretical training was necessary: 'the work here requires another level than the intellectual one [*that is the practical level*]'.

Second, there were complaints to do with curriculum subjects. For example, some elements of training was seen as irrelevant: in Germany workers referred to subjects such as organizational sciences, medical knowledge, history, statistics, children's literature methodologies, political ideology and biology, as not entirely relevant to their daily work. Some subjects were considered outmoded, for example, training completed in the former East Germany was still seen as 'dealing with the conception of man in communism' and moral themes in religion. Other workers gave examples of subjects missing from their training curriculum such as teamwork, management skills, music and arts.

Third, some workers, particularly those in England, but also some in Denmark criticized the conditions under which training had taken place. Among those mentioned were the distance travelled to access training, the fact that there was not enough training available, having to complete training in one's own time, and (in England) a lack of financial support for professional social work training. One staff member in England said that where training opportunities were tied to specific establishments, the training needs of peripatetic workers were easily forgotten.

The role of personal attributes

Training and qualification are one part of what is necessary for staff employed in residential work. At the same time, the personal attributes of staff are also important. Across different questions, many heads of establishment and staff, particularly in England, referred to the attributes required for residential work. For some, it appeared that the personal qualities of staff were their 'real' source of strength. Qualities such as the ability to cope with stressful situations, were important to 'withstand the rigours of the job', as one head put it. They also provided the main resource for workers in the absence of relevant qualifications.

The salience of personal characteristics was often acknowledged by the researchers themselves, in the fieldwork documentation. At the end of each interview schedule, there was a section which required a 'One paragraph summary of interviewer impressions (include any observations or general impressions that are not recorded elsewhere in your interview notes)'. In fact, interviewers often wrote at much greater length. They described the premises, incidents they had observed and they frequently alluded to how they themselves had experienced the personnel whom they had interviewed. We acknowledge that the accounts of the fieldworkers may well reflect national cultures and individual values as much as any 'objective' truth.

Neither these informal observations, nor the verbatim responses of staff across a range questions, were designed for quantitative analysis. Familiarity with the completed interview schedules suggested, however, that a qualitative analysis, taking note of occasions on which the personal attributes of staff were mentioned, would be worthwhile.

Notes mentioning personal attributes, made by the researchers working in England, included reference to the following terms: empathy, caring, involved, committed, assertive, thoughtful, attentive, encouraging, interested, capable, dedicated, sensitive, motherly, realistic, affectionate, competent, approachable, reassuring, positive outlook, father figure, enthusiastic, engaging, cheerful and calm.

The Danish researcher used similar terms: calm, involved, reflective, observant, quiet, engaged, relaxed, energetic, kind, open, direct and contemplative. The deputy head of a Danish children's home emphasized the importance of personality as a third 'factor that decides whether you succeed in pedagogical work' (the other two being professional education and continuous professional development). His words were recorded by the Danish researcher and translated as:

> The personality is an important part of the job here ... the feeling of well-being in the work. If you do not succeed it can be measured in frustrations, neglect, power and the [lack of] will to continue. There is a demand for many different competencies. [The pedagogue] needs to be thoughtful and analysing, at the same time critical, reflecting, original and put forward untraditional ideas. To be empathetic and at the same time have insight about yourself. To be able to realize plans of actions; to be realistic about one's own activities and personal resources. To develop visions and an orientation towards the future, what tomorrow demands; to be oriented towards process and at the same time be structured, to keep to the agenda, the timetable and the conditions of work. That is the ideal. There is always a balance and a contradiction one has to be able to embrace – to be aware of one's own weaknesses, and that it is not possible to control the world. Humility is demanded to let oneself be guided in some situations, and to take over and show the way in others. Personality has for me to come into focus. Personality and professionality go hand in hand.

This pedagogue sees personal qualities as important *in combination* with, and in order to make the best use of, reflective abilities. Another head of department in Denmark drew attention to the importance of personal qualities when he said, 'To be able to maintain this job – personally, professional and administratively – it is necessary to develop *intuition* and *a sense of the situation* – the most important elements in the work, plus theoretical knowledge' (emphasis added).

In Germany, different residential care workers were described by the researchers as: open-minded, involved, attentive, kind, friendly, energetic, reflective, thoughtful, resolute, lively and engaged in their work. One German staff member remarked that 'the human being must be at the centre' when working in residential care while another member of staff stated that to be a 'social pedagogue is not so much a profession as more a passion', with the understanding that the ability to work with human feeling – the heart is a key element in residential care (see Chapter 2).

In brief, the significance attached to what were seen as the positive personal qualities of workers was notable in all three countries. These were necessary both to help young people and to maintain the emotional integrity of staff themselves in what was described by some as a 'draining' environment. The attributes which workers brought to the job were resources both for their own further development, human and professional, and for supporting the development of the young people with whom they worked.

However, the personal attributes mentioned by interviewees were not always positive. Some English informants, both heads of establishment and staff, had concerns about staff. One head said there was 'high staff turnover and inexperienced ... poor quality staff ... staff with unrealistic views about the job'. A staff member said that some colleagues 'do it for the money, not because they want to work with young people or feel committed ... some say it's not bad pay for doing nothing – watch TV all day'. Additional dimensions of poor quality were seen in staff incapable 'of doing a professional qualification' and unable 'to be consistent' in their practice. Another worker said, 'The number of people here who really want to work with kids is disheartening, so people try to get by on a minimal amount of work'.

By contrast, very few adverse comments about the personal qualities of staff were made by the heads of Danish and German residential establishments. We do not claim that such reservations about the personal qualities of staff in English residential care were expressed frequently. We report them because they suggest that, while positive personal attributes are an important characteristic of residential care workers, to rely on recruits having such qualities is no substitute for relevant professional qualifications and training. Over-reliance on staff being able to present the specific personal resources that are necessary for their work can only be detrimental in a demanding work environment.

Commitment to working with children

Nearly all the residential care workers across the three countries reported that they were committed to continuing to work with children. Over 90 percent of staff interviewed in each country said they felt settled in their jobs. The great majority of informants would recommend residential care work to a friend (84–90 percent across the three countries). Something under a half of all (40–55 percent across countries), when asked about future plans, saw themselves remaining in residential care work, and others (20–29 percent across countries) said they would like to do further study for work with children.

Further questioning revealed that being settled in a post was mostly a result of workers being committed to other people in the establishment, to staff teams and to children and young people. Staff in Denmark particularly mentioned that they were committed to the ethos of the establishment: 61 percent compared to 8 percent of staff in Germany and 22 percent of staff in England ($p<0.001$).

What lies behind commitment?

Most of the residential care workers interviewed found their work highly rewarding, but also often difficult and stressful. Below, we examine the positive and negative aspects of the work and try to draw out any national differences and account for them. We asked staff, 'What would you say were the most positive aspects of your work with children and young people here at [name of establishment]', This was followed by probes, such as, 'What is it about the work here that you find most satisfying/rewarding? Which parts of your work do you enjoy the most?'

In Denmark, workers reported, on average, twice as many positive aspects of the work as workers in England, with the reports from workers in Germany falling in between (means 3.50 (sd=1.33) in Denmark; 2.35 (sd=1.16) in Germany; and 1.63 (sd=0.88) in England). This may suggest that the pedagogues in Danish residential care found more enjoyment in their work than workers in other countries. These differences were statistically significant ($p<0.001$).

Table 4.6 shows that there were some significant differences between the countries about rewarding aspects of the work. Among staff in England, working with children's problems was most frequently mentioned as a rewarding aspect of work (cited by 82 percent of staff). A higher proportion of staff in Denmark gave this response (90 percent) but fewer workers in German establishments did so (63 percent) ($p<0.02$).

In Germany, staff most commonly (90 percent) cited relationships with

Table 4.6: Positive aspects of their work with children and young people reported by staff: numbers and percentages

Positive aspects of the work	England N (%)	Germany N (%)	Denmark N (%)	Total N (%)
Working with children's problems:*	40 (82)	31 (63)	34 (90)	105 (77)
Relationships with the children:***	23 (47)	44 (90)	35 (92)	102 (75)
Staff relationships:***	9 (18)	15 (31)	37 (97)	61 (45)
Self-orientated: (e.g., gaining experience/qualifications):**	1 (2)	6 (12)	11 (29)	18 (13)
Working conditions (e.g., shifts, pay):*	1 (2)	8 (16)	8 (21)	17 (13)
Manager-led change:†	2 (4)	0 (0)	1 (3)	3 (2)
Ethos of establishment:†	1 (2)	3 (6)	3 (8)	7 (5)
Quality of leadership:***	0 (0)	1 (2)	12 (32)	13 (10)
Working with families:†	0 (0)	3 (6)	1 (3)	4 (3)
Other:†	3 (6)	9 (18)	4 (11)	16 (12)
No positive aspects mentioned:†	0 (0)	0 (0)	1 (3)	1 (1)
Total number of staff:	49 (100)	49 (100)	38 (100)	136 (100)
Missing cases:	5 (–)	2 (–)	1 (–)	8 (–)

Notes: † Not significant; * p<0.05; ** p<0.01; *** p<0.001. A multiple response table: staff could have mentioned more than one positive aspect of their work with children and young people. Therefore columns may not sum to 100%.

children as something they enjoyed, and these were also highly valued by staff in Denmark (92 percent), compared to 47 percent of staff in England (p<0.001).

Nearly all staff in Denmark found working with colleagues rewarding (97 percent), compared to their counterparts in England (18 percent) and Germany (31 percent) (p<0.001). For staff in Denmark this almost unanimous, unprompted response is striking and perhaps speaks of the high value placed on team work and, in wider Danish society, on social participation and collaboration.

A thematic analysis of verbatim answers to these questions picked up three other sources of reward for residential care workers. First, and across all three countries, was 'making a difference' to young people's lives: staff gained pleasure from witnessing small or large successes in the lives of young people whose optimism about life had increased. In some cases, this was spoken of as 'turning around' the lives of young people by providing them with stability and security at a daily level, with opportunities for small changes, improvements and achievements. Such changes could be in relation to helping a young person integrate into the institution: one worker in England said a positive aspect of the work was, 'when you get a really challenging child, and who is aggressive, and doesn't want to be told the rules, and gradually you calm them, and get them to almost enjoy living here, and to integrate more'.

A slightly more passive role for workers, but in a similar vein, was implied by this comment from a respondent in Germany: 'watching how the children grow up and are prepared for life' in relation, for example, to seeing a young person's pride at gaining an educational qualification, or re-establishing contact between a child and her or his mother, or observing that a return visit home 'had worked out for them'.

A second area of reward was what we might call 'companionate' rewards: the reward inherent in 'being with' young people. A conception of the worker/child relationship as an attachment relationship, as we discussed earlier, would suggest a mutual affectional bond between them, with both gaining satisfaction from the relationship, both personal and, for the member of staff, professional. A few of the workers in England referred to the reward to be had from being with young people, saying they liked the 'close one-to-one contact', 'living with the kids' and 'getting on well with young people', but companionate rewards were a particular feature of the accounts of pedagogues. Staff in Denmark and Germany drew on the idea of the 'children's life world', and the associative life of the group of residents and staff. As one pedagogue in Denmark said, 'being together is important', as the context for gaining a 'deep knowledge' of the young people whose life space they shared. Another residential worker in Denmark said that she was rewarded through being 'together with the young people, maybe not for a long time, but that we are on their side and support them … I enjoy working with them, their power, the dialogue', that is the debates that go backwards and forwards between adults and young people.

Third, features of organizational structures, the work environment and prevailing ethos, can themselves be rewarding. Very few staff in English establishments (2 percent) described working conditions as a positive aspect of their work but rather more pedagogues working in Denmark and Germany (16 percent each) did so (p<0.05). These are structures that can help pedagogues become more confident about, and conscious of, their actions in relation to young people. Ongoing training was one such feature, promoting, as one informant said, 'feelings and thoughts about the work all the time'.

According to informants in Denmark, in particular, the way management structure the working day can itself promote loyalty and a 'fruitful and constructive environment' within the staff group. One spoke of peer supervision in the evenings, regular morning and other staff meetings where '[you] are not afraid of saying when you have made mistakes' and where he could learn from colleagues. Another spoke of 'good support from colleagues, without them I would not be here'. A worker in Germany referred to what was translated as 'joyful teamwork'.

In some cases, in answer to the same question, staff related that they could exercise autonomy. Some staff in Denmark said that their ongoing professional development was linked to the opportunities they had for introducing new ideas into the 'structure and frameworks' of their establishments. They believed that this demonstrated respect for their critical thinking and professional autonomy. A pedagogue illustrated this: 'if you have ideas and you can give the reasons, why then you have possibilities to work and change'. The sense that in Denmark pedagogues worked in democratically oriented institutions, where tasks and responsibilities were delegated, went hand in hand with their undertaking a wide range of responsibilities, as we shall see later. One pedagogue said she gained much from working in an institution where education, training and a 'professional orientation' were emphasized and presented challenges: 'It is a challenge to work with staff groups and to be able to take decisions and be a leader'. And another said: 'It is a house where it is good to be; you are recognized and tasks are delegated'.

Dissatisfaction with residential care work

In order to obtain other indications of the level of staff satisfaction with residential care, we asked, 'Are you thinking of leaving this job at all?' and, where they were thinking of leaving, we asked about their reasons. Their answers are set out in Table 4.7.

A quarter or more of all staff cited dissatisfaction with pay and/or working conditions as the reason (or one of the reasons) they wished to leave. When salary (converted to purchasing power parity values (PPP)) was taken into account, between country differences in pay were not significant (p=0.7).

Stress was the next most commonly cited factor among those wishing to leave (18 percent, overall). Significantly more staff in Germany (51 percent) cited personal and domestic issues as a reason for leaving, compared to 22 percent in Denmark and 8 percent in England (p<0.001).

It is especially worth noting that few informants said they wished to leave their current post for reasons connected with the young people living in the establishments or with their families – although, throughout the interviews, there were many indications that these could be sources of stress. This would seem to indicate, at least on the basis of their own reports, strong staff commitment to the young people and to working with them.

We also asked residential care staff about the least positive aspects of their current work with children and young people. Only five of the staff interviewed identified no negative aspects of their work. For those who had criticisms, 13 negative aspects of work were identified (see Table 4.8), ranging from client-centred to job-oriented and organizational issues. Where staff identified any negative aspects of the work, those most mentioned were as follows. For the residential workers in England, working with children's

Table 4.7:   Responses to the question, 'Are you thinking of leaving this job at all?': numbers and percentages

Response	England N (%)	Germany N (%)	Denmark N (%)	Total N (%)
The pay and working conditions:†	12 (25)	13 (28)	12 (32)	37 (28)
Emotional and/or physical stress:†	9 (19)	11 (23)	4 (11)	24 (18)
The children and young people:†	5 (10)	3 (6)	5 (14)	13 (10)
Personal/domestic reasons:**	4 (8)	24 (51)	8 (22)	36 (27)
The management:†	4 (8)	0 (0)	4 (11)	8 (6)
Staff issues:†	4 (8)	2 (4)	3 (8)	9 (7)
The ethos of the establishment:†	3 (6)	3 (6)	6 (16)	12 (9)
Working with other agencies:†	3 (6)	0 (0)	1 (3)	4 (3)
Career development:†	2 (4)	6 (13)	5 (13)	13 (10)
Administrative duties:†	2 (4)	0 (0)	0 (0)	2 (2)
The families:†	0 (0)	1 (2)	1 (3)	2 (2)
Externally imposed change:*	0 (0)	0 (0)	4 (11)	4 (3)
Other reasons:†	4 (8)	1 (2)	1 (3)	6 (5)
Not thinking of leaving:†	17 (35)	7 (15)	9 (24)	33 (25)
Total number of staff:	48 (100)	47 (100)	37 (100)	132 (–)
Missing cases:	6 (–)	4 (–)	2 (–)	12 (–)

Notes: † Not significant; * p<0.01; ** p<0.001. A multiple response table: staff could have mentioned more than one reason for thinking of leaving their jobs. Therefore columns may not sum to 100%.

problems was most frequently mentioned (by 29 percent of staff), followed next by working conditions (25 percent) and then by working with other agencies (11 percent). For staff in Germany, relationships with children were mentioned as a negative aspect of the work by 26 percent of staff, followed by working with children's problems (26 percent) and, third, by more general working conditions (24 percent). For informants in Denmark, the negative aspect of work mentioned most frequently was lack of resources (by 24 percent of staff), followed by working conditions (mentioned by 19 percent of staff), with difficulties arising in work with other agencies, and difficulties that arose in the course of work with parents (both mentioned by 14 percent of staff).

Between country differences, as to the aspects of their work that staff experienced as negative, reached statistical significance on the following items: staff in Denmark were significantly more likely than those in England or Germany to report that they were insufficiently resourced (p<0.005); and workers in German establishments were significantly more likely to report relationships with young people as a negative aspect of the work: 26 percent compared to 15 percent of those in England and 3 percent in Denmark (p<0.01).

Table 4.8: Negative aspects of work with children and young people: numbers and percentages

Negative aspects of the work	England N (%)	Germany N (%)	Denmark N (%)	Total N (%)
Client-centred				
Working with children's problems:†	13 (29)	13 (24)	3 (8)	35 (27)
Relationships with the children:**	7 (15)	13 (26)	1 (3)	21 (16)
Lack of progress with young people:†	1 (2)	6 (12)	3 (8)	10 (8)
Working with parents:*	0 (0)	3 (6)	5 (14)	8 (6)
Violence:†	3 (6)	1 (2)	1 (3)	5 (4)
Job-oriented				
Working conditions (e.g., shifts, pay):†	11 (25)	12 (24)	7 (19)	30 (23)
Self-orientated (e.g., gaining experience/qualifications):†	2 (4)	3 (6)	1 (3)	6 (5)
Organizational issues				
Resources:**	2 (4)	3 (6)	9 (24)	14 (11)
Staff relationships:†	4 (8)	7 (14)	1 (3)	12 (9)
Bureaucracy:†	4 (9)	5 (10)	3 (8)	12 (9)
Working with other agencies:†	5 (11)	2 (4)	5 (14)	12 (9)
Management:†	9 (4)	0 (0)	3 (8)	7 (5)
Practical work: (e.g., cleaning):†	3 (7)	1 (2)	3 (8)	7 (5)
Other:†	5 (11)	6 (12)	3 (8)	14 (11)
No negative aspects mentioned:†	2 (4)	1 (2)	2 (5)	5 (4)
Total:	44 (100)	50 (100)	37 (100)	131 (100)
Missing cases:	10 (–)	1 (–)	2 (–)	13 (–)

Notes: † Not significant; * $p<0.05$; ** $p<0.01$. A multiple response table: staff could have mentioned more than one reason negative aspect of working with children and young people. Therefore columns may not sum to 100%.

It is perhaps worth drawing attention here to the concern, predominantly expressed by workers in England, about violence directed towards themselves. For example, one informant said they did not enjoy, 'being physically attacked, and physical violence and verbal abuse'. Another said she did not like seeing, 'colleagues being attacked' but she herself, 'diffused things, I miss out on punches'. Another explained that physical assaults could lead to contact with the police, with sometimes serious consequences for the young person concerned; this could also create dilemmas for staff. Staff asked themselves if they had done the right thing in reporting violent incidents to police. Could they have done something else? In one English establishment a care worker reported that the 'least positive' aspect of residential care was:

> Having to report people to the police about behaviour here or out-
> side, because they [the children] have had a raw deal. I won't be
> assaulted or allow criminal damage, if it's got that far. What I've done
> may be lacking, despite my knowledge, and skills. [It] would be nice
> if there was something else, some other way of controlling kids.
> Particularly with ten year olds. One deliberately went and assaulted a
> member of staff and [was] racially abusive, nothing else we could do
> but report it. We have the right not to be hit and have the home
> wrecked.

Only three workers in Germany and Denmark commented on physical
force or violence as negative aspects of the job in answering the question
about negative aspects of work with children and young people. Two of these
responses were in relation to staff members themselves having to use physical
force to control a child; another pedagogue, however, said the level of physical threat had once been such that he had 'feared for his life'.

The sometimes emotional burden entailed in residential care was occasionally commented on by workers in Denmark. For example, pedagogues
said that young people could be very demanding, they could be over-
dependent on staff members and that they sometimes reverted to earlier
behaviour patterns. One pedagogue said:

> You can feel very drained because of the problems of the children
> and of witnessing how tragic their fates are ... to see a child very
> unhappy and sad and there [is] no prospect that [their] mother will
> have a better situation or improve. It touches you. Sometimes, no
> matter how much you give or fill in, then you cannot fill these
> children up. There is still a gap [or] void and they crave for more. The
> days when you are not bursting with energy you may get a feeling of
> fatigue.

To summarize, the residential care workers in all three countries reported
being highly committed to working with young people. Overall, the rewards
of the work outweigh the sources of dissatisfaction. In England, however,
workers reported concerns about children's problems and the frequency with
which they faced physical violence from residents.

Recruitment and retention

Next we turn to issues of staff recruitment and retention: obtaining sufficient
and appropriate staff, and the length of time they remain in post, once
recruited. These issues are linked to aspects of job satisfaction and commit-

ment, such as those described above, alongside other considerations. Other factors that affect staff recruitment and retention include the state of the local or national economy; job conditions, for example when an employer finances training, on condition that workers stay in post; highly specialized qualifications that restrict occupational mobility; the availability of alternative employment; and domestic circumstances that constrain occupational choices.

Issues of recruitment and retention were a major focus of comments made by heads of establishments in England, but much less so in Denmark and Germany. A high level of turnover in care services is often said to be indicative of poor quality care and poor quality employment (Cost, Quality and Child Outcomes Study Team 1995; Whitebook et al. 1989). Lower turnover, the recruitment of good applicants, good working conditions and a high quality of care appear to go hand in hand.

Recruitment issues in England

Recruiting staff was reported to be very difficult for heads of establishments in England (88 percent said there were problems finding staff), but less so in Germany (46 percent) and not at all in Denmark (p<0.001). Given the prevalence of recruitment difficulties in England we now focus on discussing the difficulties in this country, drawing on examples from the other two countries to illustrate what, reportedly, made it easier for them to recruit staff.

Heads of English establishments predicted that recruitment difficulties would become even more acute in the near to medium term. Eight heads in England attributed this to a general shortage of suitably qualified candidates (31 percent). Many heads gave multiple reasons for this. Two commonly cited reasons were: working conditions (34 percent), and the status of the work (18 percent) both within social work and as portrayed in the media. One head of establishment summed it up as: 'money, hours and how people see residential social workers'. Appointing 'good people' is hard, concluded one head, remarking that a flexible approach is required such as a willingness to 'grow your own' staff, through training programmes so they work 'to our ways', and offering support for job applicants to complete ongoing training.

Recruitment issues in Germany

In Germany, heads who faced recruitment difficulties (46 percent of all) related these to working conditions (70 percent), difficulties in obtaining properly qualified staff (30 percent), low status (18 percent), low pay (14 percent) and the availability of alternative, attractive work (14 percent).

Successful recruitment

In England, heads of establishment said that success in recruiting staff derived from having a good reputation locally, having high staff ratios and having a safe place to work. Some private and voluntary sector heads, with establishments owned by larger organizations, said pooling resources and recruiting by the central organization helped considerably. One head reported that she interviewed 'people in a two stage process, they are taken round units and do two trial shifts and get a feel for the job. So here you get a chance to get a feel of what the job is like, [they] can make up their minds'. Several heads of establishment commented on the risks inherent in not choosing the right staff: 'you can't afford to get it wrong. I have made mistakes in the past and you need to follow gut feeling'. Another head said one had to 'spot the person who is particularly good', assessing their skills not just in interviews, but also in how they participated in a group.

Successful recruitment strategies employed in England were also reported by heads of establishment in Denmark and Germany. For example, the manager of a large Danish establishment summarized why she found it easy to recruit new staff:

> The institution has a close position near to the training centre for pedagogues. It has a good reputation. Recently, there were more than 80 well-qualified applicants for six vacancies. Applicants can come from positions like deputies in day care centres for 100 children. There is a big interest in working in this specific area, the interest for the children. Residential care appeals to many: the reputation is very good; [there are] parties for the staff and they get on together very well; word of mouth method. The institution is well-known for having reflected on its professionalism, through books published about their methods.

In both Germany and Denmark, having a good supply of pedagogically trained people available for work, as well as some local unemployment, made recruiting staff less of a problem than in England. Heads of establishment in Denmark also said the challenging nature of the work was itself an attraction and that good working conditions and the high status of the work made recruiting easy. However, some saw early signs of problems. Recruiting male staff, integrating new staff into established staff groups, conditions such as shift work, relatively low salaries, and high levels of work-related stress were all cited as difficulties.

Staff retention

As with recruitment, issues surrounding staff retention are complex and dynamic, involving combinations of factors including working conditions, personal characteristics and the national and local economic background. Difficulty retaining staff in post was largely reported as an English phenomenon: 46 percent of the managers interviewed in England found keeping staff difficult, compared to 8 percent in Germany and none in Denmark (p<0.005). These accounts were reflected in managers' reports of residential care staff turnover in the year preceding the research interview: reportedly 10 percent of staff in Danish establishments, compared with 18 percent in German establishments and 27 percent in the English residential homes visited[3].

Retaining staff in England

Given that English managers were more likely to express difficulties with staff recruitment, this section again focuses on data from England, before moving on to discuss, across all three countries, strategies for supporting staff in post.

In England, similar factors to those that made it difficult to recruit staff were reported to make it difficult to keep them: pay, conditions of work and the poor image of social work in the media. As one head said, 'It's a thankless task. Pay and conditions make it difficult to survive in London. Opportunities for promotion are not always there'. Moreover, the work itself was hard: 'Staff [are] on [their] knees: up at 3am, on sleep over, then start [work again] at 7.30am'. Shift work and overnight duties were said to combine badly with family responsibilities: 'Sleeping away from home, weekend work, people with families want to be off when their children are off, but we need them here then'. Staff were said to get 'burned out quickly' and, in addition, what were seen as bureaucratic demands were increasing. One manager remarked: 'More demands without human resources, it's being seen to be doing, rather than actually doing'. Another said that staff were being asked 'to do an impossible task, to spend all [the] time with children, and write it down at the same time [i.e., keep records].

Keeping staff with the 'right' personal attributes to work in the 'tough' environment of residential care was seen as important by some heads. They said that staff had to have 'good personal levels of resilience' and 'inner strengths' in order to succeed, and, without this, as one head remarked, staff leave: they 'come into it for the wrong reasons, so they won't stay. [They] come in for money and think it's an easy ride, and [they] don't have to work hard'.

Some groups of workers were seen as having only short-term commitment to residential care. For example, there were male workers said to be *en route* to better paid management jobs, who 'feel they can do better in other sectors and earn more'. Conversely, younger, well-educated women were reportedly gaining work experience before going on to social work or other professional qualifications. More generally, heads reported that they 'trained up' new recruits only to find that, with better qualifications and experience, staff departed to better paid jobs with more congenial conditions.

At the same time, serious concerns were expressed by some of the English heads about the poor quality of some staff, who, as one said, 'can't work anywhere else, who lack vision, with high sickness, many inter-staff disputes, and [about whom there are] complaints from young people'.

Another factor to be reported by heads of English establishments was a perceived rise in the level of violence among young people. Nine of the 13 heads of English establishments who reported difficulties in retaining staff said that violent behaviour among young people in residential care was becoming more commonplace. In the past, mainstream school attendance and participation in organized activities were reported to have been the norm in children's homes. By the time of our fieldwork, this was said to have been replaced with a new set of norms: young people with criminal records, rising levels of violence among residents, increasing numbers of assaults on staff, more absconding from the home and drug abuse, often related to other criminal activity. One head described her clientele as, 'All boys who have been excluded from school, all abused, all offenders, previously involved in domestic violence. Boys who had left [their] mums and been attacking mums'.

Measures to support staff and improve retention

We also asked managers who found it easy to retain staff, why this was so. Table 4.9 shows many between country differences. For example, heads of establishments in Germany and Denmark were more likely than those in England to put forward favourable working conditions and congenial work, as influential in retaining staff. In Denmark more managers than in the other countries reported that the characteristics intrinsic to residential work are important: it is valuable and rewarding work and staff enjoy working with children. In England, the most frequently cited factor affecting staff retention was that the work was rewarding (5/16).

Table 4.9: Grounds given by heads of establishment for finding it easy to retain staff: numbers and percentages

	England N (%)	Germany N (%)	Denmark N (%)	Total N (%)
Pay:†	4 (25)	2 (18)	3 (27)	9 (24)
Working conditions:*	3 (19)	7 (64)	5 (46)	15 (40)
Valuable work:**	2 (13)	0 (0)	5 (46)	7 (18)
Other available work not attractive:*	0 (0)	1 (9)	3 (27)	4 (11)
Congenial work:*	3 (19)	6 (55)	4 (36)	13 (34)
Rewarding work:†	5 (31)	1 (9)	4 (36)	10 (26)
Staff like working with children:***	1 (6)	1 (9)	6 (55)	8 (21)
Other reason:†	13 (81)	8 (73)	5 (46)	26 (68)
Total:	16 (100)	11 (100)	11 (100)	38 (100)
Missing cases:	9 (–)	8 (–)	1 (–)	18 (–)

Notes: † Not significant; * p<0.05; ** p<0.01; *** p<0.001. A multiple response table: heads could have mentioned more than one reason for finding it easy to retain staff. Therefore columns may not sum to 100%.

Management ethos

In English homes, management style or ethos was cited as having a major impact on staff retention. Six English heads reported that, in order to support staff, they had to provide a clear 'focus and direction' for the work, and 'management systems for staff to feel they [the staff] are in charge'. A similar proportion spoke of the central importance of valuing the staff team: they 'feel that they're valued, consulted, they feel as if their contribution is valid and playing a major role', with open communication systems, including regular supervision, and staff feeling they 'can speak about how they feel about the children' in staff meetings.

Some heads of establishments took the view that staff should have delegated authority. At the same time, they thought that managers should be available '24 hours a day ... this access to managers helps everyone, no real separation [between staff and management], and the manager does things when needed ... so [the] kids know you'. Others reported having 'team meetings and development days' which help to make the staff group more consistent and cohesive.

Among heads of English establishments who thought they were successful in retaining staff were those who ensured that rota systems were flexible and took account of workers' childcare needs, and those who had instituted a regular staff training programme. Two heads of establishments referred to having developed their own 'banks' of workers, on which they could draw to cover staff absences. In this way they could make use of a familiar group of regularly used staff, in preference to employing staff from expensive and impersonal agencies.

The positive effect of wider policy measures

Despite some concerns about bureaucracy invading practice, many heads of establishments in England saw the emerging policy environment as helping to retain staff through signalling a greater government interest in residential care. One head said that, 'having targets, goals . . . [for] the care of young people and discussions which lead to better outcomes for them . . . encourages staff and increases satisfaction'. Similarly, having targets for acquiring qualifications promised more of a career in children's care, rather, as one head put it, than being seen as 'baby minders'. These measures, as another said, 'give direction' to practice and help stop staff being 'sucked into young people's behaviour'.

Being part of a wider organization (whether public or private) was also seen as helpful by some heads, so long as they retained their autonomy and could refuse to admit certain young people. One referred to her multi-disciplinary context: 'I'm well supported here in terms of management, and consultations with a psychiatric unit for the staff team, we get guidance'. Having a designated teacher with 'one foot in SSD [social services] and one in Education, helps with the problems of funding provision for young people'.

Finally, financial security and protected employment to be found in the public sector was seen as a staff retention measure: one head said: 'If this was the private sector a lot of staff would be thrown out because of the high sickness rates'.

Measures to support retention in Denmark and Germany

The discourse of heads of Danish and German establishments concerning staff retention focused on a holistic approach to the work environment. A head of a German establishment said that the staff had been there for a long time, they liked the work and, he wrote in capital letters on his questionnaire, 'We are a good establishment'.

The main aim expressed by heads in Germany and Denmark was to develop and sustain an ethos of staff professionality: cooperation, loyalty and teamwork, developing 'a sense of community' and a 'culture of involvement'. A manager in Germany said that it was important to take good care of staff, and saw this in terms of including staff in decision-making, the delegation of tasks to staff, selecting staff teams well and providing staff with a high level of individual flexibility. The same interviewee spoke of the professional standards of the establishment. Professionality was described as having a confidence in the skills, knowledge and capacities of a pedagogue. Managers had to achieve a 'clear and unambiguous leadership with respect for all staff', which would in turn produce staff cooperation. In Denmark, a head of establishment said:

> I emphasize above all [that staff should] be professional, and believe in their own professionality, and this leads to cooperation. This is a job, and the relations between staff must be based upon that [professionality]. That well-being must build on loyalty to one's colleagues and the work itself.

Furthermore, managers in Germany and Denmark said they had to instil among staff the idea that the work is 'meaningful', and what both the individual and the staff team as a whole do is 'important work', and that 'the management gives feedback to it [reinforces this understanding]'. Management for their part should:

> Take a real interest in the staff as the human beings they are (we ask if they have been ill, about their children, parents, etc.), but with 60 staff members it has become more difficult to see each as persons. The team leaders are very attentive to taking into consideration wishes when working hours are planned. We comfort each other (e.g., when relatives have died), we emphasize that consideration is given to private life. This leads to mutuality. That we within the staff try to live out the attitudes that we have, to the children living in this institution, and to their parents.
>
> (Manager of a Danish establishment)

Developing staff skills and autonomy was seen as important for workers' participation in management. For example, in some residential homes in Denmark, staff members participated in recruitment processes for new staff so that, as one manager said, 'they experience that they have autonomy . . . and a responsibility and . . . they think they would not have [that] in other residential institutions'.

Attention to the professional work environment was argued by Danish managers to have

> created an attractive working environment where all feel heard and respected and with a good possibility to develop. There is a wide liberty of action for the individual staff . . . we work with both their personal and their professional development [and this] has led to . . . extra energy for the job.

As a result, heads reported that pedagogues preferred to work with a challenging clientele of young people rather than in universal services because 'they want to grasp or touch deeper layers ... they stay here because of the challenges which they [also] experience as difficult and frustrating'.

In summary, reports on staff retention from German and Danish heads of establishments differ from those in England in several ways: the client group is defined more positively; the staff group is defined as more skilful, resourceful, autonomous and reflective; the job of pedagogue is defined as more attractive; and residential care is defined in terms of success at helping young people rather than dogged survival in the face of constant criticism.

Discussion

In England and many other countries, policy aspirations for children in residential care have moved far beyond providing food, shelter and protection. In all the countries we studied, national policies intend residential care settings to promote children's well-being and competence. If they are to succeed in this, the workforce for residential care must play a major role: it has to be sufficient both in number and equipped and supported to carry out a demanding job. This chapter has documented workforce issues in residential care in England, Denmark and Germany. We have explored the working environment in contemporary residential children's care in terms of the characteristics of staff, their initial and ongoing training, their commitment to the work, together with turnover, recruitment and retention issues. In many respects, we found that the English establishments, and their workforce, were at a disadvantage compared with their continental counterparts, in these matters.

There were wide differences in the extent to which staff held a relevant formal qualification and in the level at which it was pitched, with English residential homes having more workers with lower level qualifications while nearly all the workers in Denmark had a high level qualification, as did half of the staff in German establishments, with the other half having a medium level qualification. With regard to staff turnover, recruitment and retention, these were clearly of greater concern in England, with higher turnover and more difficulties reported in recruiting and retaining staff. Compared with the other two countries, English heads of homes were very concerned about poor working conditions and the low status of residential care work. Recruiting and keeping staff is perhaps the central issue for English heads of homes, for without this there is no service for young people. Danish establishments reported fewest problems with the recruitment and retention of staff. This is especially interesting given that, in Denmark, employment for qualified pedagogues is available in widespread universal services, such as nurseries and out-of-school services.

Findings from Germany and Denmark suggest that the level and extent of initial and continuing professional education; having an organizational ethos to which staff express high levels of commitment; holding 'being together' with children and young people as a value in its own right; and providing structures, events and professional alliances that make 'being together' as a staff group stimulating and attractive to staff: all, in combination, appear to slow the rate of staff vacancies and lead to an increasing take up of vacancies when these become available.

For all the workers, both the rewards and sources of dissatisfaction in residential care centred on making a difference to young people's lives. For workers in England, this was focused on achieving a positive outcome for young people, while for staff in Denmark and Germany, there were also many references to 'being together' with young people. That is they felt positive about situations that provided opportunities for attachment between young people and themselves. These accounts are consistent with the relational approach to caregiving that Crouter and colleagues' (2005) research with parents indicated is protective for young people.

It is also striking that residential care workers in all three countries reported a high level of commitment to the work, in spite of the challenges that the work presented. Reports of violence featured frequently in the English accounts, much less so in the accounts from Germany and Denmark. Again across all countries, staff were highly appreciative of in-service and other training opportunities, although these appeared to be at a lower and more instrumental level in England than in the other countries. Together, these findings suggest the potential of the English workforce for professional development: staff in England like and are committed to work in residential care, while at the same time they appreciate and enjoy training opportunities.

Notes

1   It is important to note when reading the data findings reported in this chapter, that some data were missing for some of the managers and residential care workers interviewed. Data were missing from some heads of establishment due to incomplete questionnaire responses in some instances, and to establishment characteristics – for example, some units did not have any residents aged 16 and over. In addition, seven German unit managers completed questionnaires but were not interviewed – the head of the whole establishment was interviewed instead – and these cases have been treated as missing for all analyses involving head interview data. Also, eight staff (one from England, one from Germany and six from Denmark) were interviewed

but did not complete a questionnaire, and five staff (three in England, one in Germany and one in Denmark) completed a questionnaire, but were not interviewed. The total number of cases (the 'N') on which our statistical analyses are based differs accordingly (for analysis of staff data, for example, 139 cases are included in analysis of *interview* items, and 136 cases in the analysis of *questionnaire* items only). As a consequence, numbers – and hence statistical power – were limited for some analyses, and are reported for each analysis separately.

2   SEDOC is a common frame of reference for training and work placement adopted by the European Community in 1985. It is composed of five levels, defined by duration of training and level at which it is pitched. For the purposes of this analysis, we have used three levels (grouping together levels 2, 3 and 4), which in our view provides sufficient differentiation while avoiding over-complexity.

3   In 2003, overall employee turnover in the UK was 16 percent, and 10 percent among public sector workers (CIPD 2004).

5 Understandings and values: orientations to practice among staff

In the last chapter we drew on findings from our second study, which looked in some detail at practice in residential establishments in Denmark, Germany and England. It examined characteristics, qualifications and training in the residential homes studied, before going on to consider the ease with which establishments were able to recruit and retain staff.

In this chapter, we consider whether there are distinctive approaches to working with children in residential care in each of these three countries. Again we draw on data from the second study. In particular we will look at staff responsibilities towards young people, how they think about the children they work with and the various approaches they adopt in working with children.

Roles and responsibilities

Our analysis revealed that, as with other studies of the residential care role (Berridge and Brodie 1998; Sinclair and Gibbs 1998), staff undertook many and varied responsibilities and tasks (see Table 5.1). In all three countries, residential care staff interviewed were involved in administrative tasks such as record keeping (around 74 percent of all respondents) and liaison with other professionals and agencies (62 percent of respondents). However, there were important cross-national differences.

Across all three countries, while most staff were responsible for day-to-day work with one particular group of young people (83 percent overall), staff in Germany were significantly less likely to be involved with one group of young people only, compared to staff in the other two countries (71 percent) (p<0.03). Many respondents in each country were key workers, taking designated responsibilities for one or more young people, but staff in England were less likely to be key workers than their counterparts in Denmark and Germany (49 percent in England, compared with 71 percent in Germany, and 74 percent in Denmark) (p<0.03). Finally, residential care staff in Denmark were more likely than English and German workers to be responsible for working with parents (71 percent of staff in Denmark, compared with 51 percent in Germany and 31 percent in England) (p<0.001).

Table 5.1 also shows other, less common, staff responsibilities. These include supervising other workers; being responsible for particular art and sport activities, with staff in Germany more likely to report responsibility in this area (England, 10 percent; Denmark, 18 percent; and Germany, 33 percent); and other management tasks and responsibilities. Pedagogues in Denmark reported a wider range of responsibilities than workers in the other two countries.

Table 5.1: Reported responsibilities of staff in the establishment by country, numbers and percentages

	England N (%)	Germany N (%)	Denmark N (%)	Total N (%)
Daily responsibility for a particular group of young people:*	45 (88)	35 (71)	34 (90)	114 (83)
Administrative tasks such as record keeping:†	35 (69)	36 (74)	31 (82)	102 (74)
Liaison with other agencies/ professionals:†	26 (51)	33 (67)	26 (68)	85 (62)
Key worker for one or more individual young people:*	25 (49)	35 (71)	28 (74)	88 (64)
Liaison with families:†	16 (31)	25 (51)	27 (71)	68 (49)
Particular methods of working or interventions:†	7 (14)	9 (18)	9 (24)	25 (18)
Particular activities (e.g., swimming, art, sports):*	5 (10)	16 (33)	7 (18)	28 (20)
Management, including pedagogic management:†	4 (8)	8 (16)	7 (18)	19 (14)
Domestic work:†	4 (8)	4 (8)	0 (0)	8 (6)
Working in teams:†	0 (0)	2 (4)	0 (0)	2 (1)
Responsibility for students:*	0 (0)	0 (0)	3 (8)	3 (2)
Staff supervision:†	7 (14)	2 (4)	3 (8)	12 (9)
Other:†	4 (8)	7 (14)	4 (11)	15 (11)
Total number of cases:	51 (100)	49 (100)	38 (100)	138 (100)
Missing cases:	3 (–)	2 (–)	1 (–)	6 (–)

Notes: † Not significant; * p<0.05. A multiple response table: staff could have mentioned more than one responsibility. Therefore columns may not sum to 100%.

In both Denmark and Germany, the establishments visited were larger than in England (see Chapter 6). They also provided a significantly wider range of services (such as day care, community outreach, home visiting and schools offering places for non-resident children) than English homes. These differences were reflected in staffing levels. Including staff on full- and part-time contracts and agency staff: Danish homes visited had an average of 52 direct care staff, while the German homes had an average of 45 and English homes had 21 staff on average. Across all countries, those homes with smaller numbers of staff had fewer services on offer. From the point of view of staff, this may mean that those working in smaller homes with fewer services have less scope to develop skills, and therefore careers, than those working in larger homes.

Emotional support

A key role for staff working with children in residential care is, or should be, supporting them through difficult events and processes. This is one function of caregiving, whether by parents, foster parents or residential workers. It entails questions of how a child is 'looked after' and putting in place the means to achieve a successful upbringing for young people. In residential settings these are responsibilities that are delegated to staff, and in England, such questions are often tied to the notion of the local authority's 'corporate parenting' responsibility for children in public care.

In this section we focus, in particular, on ways of offering emotional support to young people, something that all residential workers said was part of their responsibility. The great majority of staff said that they had offered emotional support to a resident during the week before they were interviewed (81 percent in England; 96 percent in Germany; 87 percent in Denmark). Emotional support had been offered in response to a wide range of events, including those relating to criminal behaviour, family relationships, difficulties in school and relationships with other young people. Of these events, the most frequently mentioned concerned relationships with family members (41 percent overall), followed by relationships with other residents and with non-resident peers (both of whom were mentioned by 13 percent of interviewees).

Informants were asked to reflect on the last time they had provided emotional support to a young person and were then asked, 'What did you do?' on that occasion. In Table 5.2 we document the ways in which workers reported helping young people with their problems. The table shows many differences between countries, all statistically significant. For staff in Denmark, listening to the young person was an almost universal response (97 percent compared to 56 percent of German and 39 percent of English staff); this was closely followed by 'putting words to their feelings' (89 percent compared to 18 percent of German staff and 2 percent of English). These are both key features of the pedagogic approach. In England and Germany, the most commonly reported response was to have discussed or talked about difficulties (74 percent and 66 percent respectively; in Denmark staff had done so in 53 percent of cases).

Few staff in England said that they had provided physical comfort through cuddling the young person (8 percent, compared to 20 percent in Germany and 32 percent in Denmark). More staff in Denmark (60 percent) said they had spent time with the young person, as a means of offering support, than was reported in England (24 percent) or Germany (22 percent). Also, more staff interviewed in Denmark (47 percent) said they suggested to the young person strategies for dealing with the difficulties, compared with 31 percent of English workers and 20 percent in Germany.

Table 5.2:   Staff reporting how they offered young people emotional support (last occasion): numbers and percentages

	England N (%)	Germany N (%)	Denmark N (%)	Total N (%)
Discussed/ talked with them:†	36 (74)	33 (66)	20 (53)	89 (65)
Listened:**	19 (39)	28 (56)	37 (97)	84 (61)
Gave strategies for dealing with situation:*	15 (31)	10 (20)	18 (47)	43 (31)
Companionship (e.g., spent time with them):***	12 (24)	11 (22)	23 (60)	46 (34)
Referral to external agency:*	7 (14)	0 (0)	5 (13)	12 (9)
Cuddled them:*	4 (8)	10 (20)	12 (32)	26 (19)
Reference to rules or procedures:†	4 (8)	0 (0)	2 (5)	6 (4)
Talked them round to do what staff thought was best:†	3 (6)	2 (4)	2 (5)	7 (5)
Put words to their feelings:**	1 (2)	9 (18)	34 (89)	44 (32)
Other:†	13 (26)	17 (34)	8 (21)	38 (27)
Not known:†	0 (0)	0 (0)	0 (0)	0 (0)
Total number of cases:	49 (100)	50 (100)	38 (100)	137 (100)
Missing cases:	5 (–)	1 (–)	1 (–)	7 (–)

Notes: † Not significant; * p<0.05; ** p<0.001. A multiple response table: staff could have reported more than one way they offered young people emotional support. Therefore columns may not sum to 100%.

The responses show distinctive differences between staff in the three countries, which we analysed further. We next organized the different responses into three distinctive groups, each describing a particular type of approach to responding to young people in distress:

1   First, there was what might be described as an *empathic* approach. This comprised the following four categories: listening to the young

person, naming their feelings, cuddling them and companionship (spending time with the young person and being together with them when they were undertaking potentially distressing tasks). The approach is essentially child-centred, focusing on the child's feelings and having its origins in a personal relationship.

2   Second, there was a *discursive* approach. This comprised three categories: discussing/talking, suggesting strategies that might alleviate the difficulty and attempting to persuade the young person as to what staff thought best. This approach is more cognitively based, it invites, or provides, reflection and it may, to some extent, be based more in the perspective of the member of staff, than the empathic approach.

3   Third, there were *procedural* and *organizational* approaches. These involved referring the young person to the establishment's rules and procedures (for example, making plain that overnight visits to their family home needed prior agreement), reference to an external agency (putting the resident in touch with a counselling service, for example), obtaining information for the young person, or taking other action on their behalf, such as re-organizing a schedule or having a conversation with a teacher).

Table 5.3:   Staff report of type of emotional support offered to young people (last occasion): mean scores

	England: Mean number (sd)	Denmark: Mean number (sd)	Germany: Mean number (sd)	Total: Mean number (sd)
Empathic:*	0.18 (0.18)	0.71 (0.21)	0.31 (0.25)	0.37 (0.31)
Discursive:†	0.35 (0.28)	0.36 (0.32)	0.30 (0.23)	0.34 (0.28)
Procedural:†	0.08 (0.29)	0.05 (0.23)	0.00 (0.00)	0.04 (0.21)
Organizational:†	0.27 (0.49)	0.18 (0.39)	0.14 (0.35)	0.20 (0.42)

Notes: † Not significant; * $p < 0.001$. The totals for each row were divided by the number of items – empathic was comprised of four items, discursive was made up of three items, and procedural and organizational both comprised of one item. The first two: empathic and discursive were analysed using ANOVA, and the last two were analysed using Kruskal-Wallis.

For each cluster of responses we obtained a mean score per cluster for staff in each country (see Table 5.3). The aim was to compare the relative frequency of each type of response, within and between countries. Comparing means, procedural and organizational responses were reported by fewer workers overall, and between country differences were non-significant. Workers interviewed in Denmark were much more likely than those in England to say they had employed an empathic approach in responding to young people, while the mean for staff in Germany lay between those of the other two countries. These differences are statistically significant (p<0.001).

Staff in all three countries reported a similar level of *discursive support* in the three countries, with no statistically significant differences (for England, the mean was 0.35; for Germany, 0.30; and for Denmark, 0.35).

Looking at the findings in another way, workers in England most frequently reported that, when young people needed emotional support, they employed a discursive approach, with empathic approaches ranking second. For pedagogues in Germany and Denmark, on the other hand, empathic approaches were ranked highest, followed by a discursive approach.

The approach of pedagogues in Denmark was distinctive in its higher levels of both empathic emotional support approaches *and* discursive approaches, than in the other countries. This means that staff in Denmark both listened and talked, were open to young people's feelings and responded actively, they provided affirmation of young people's sense of self *and* supported their further development.

This analysis of staff accounts of their emotional support strategies highlights important cross-national differences: emotional support is a daily responsibility for staff, but among staff groups with a high level of pedagogic education, a non-directive, empathic 'listening' approach was more likely to be in evidence, combined with more discursive and reflective methods. This finding is consistent with what we know of the education of pedagogues (see Chapter 2), based on a holistic view of the child in which feelings and cognitive processes are both important. As noted in Chapter 4, nearly all (94 percent) informants in Denmark were trained to a high or degree level, compared to about half of the pedagogues working in German children's homes. In line with these qualification differences, staff in Germany also reported empathic support more than discursive support – but reported using both to a lesser degree than workers in Denmark. Only a fifth of the staff interviewed in England had a relevant degree (which, of course, was not in pedagogy) for the work in which they were employed, and they were least likely to use an empathic, non-directive response.

Among the English staff, a discursive approach was more prominent: on the whole they appeared to give less priority to children and young people as emotional beings, their relationship seemed to be based more on words and less on personal feelings and identifying with the young person. While there is a place for words, we would argue – in line with Mein's conception of 'mind-mindedness' (discussed in Chapter 1) – young people in residential care also need to be supported at the level of their feelings, and this should be a prerequisite for any discursive, reflective work with them.

There is also some evidence, from responses to a different question, of cross-country differences in the way in which staff employed a discursive approach. When asked if it was part of their work to advise young people, most staff said that it was (94 percent in England; 90 percent in Germany; 100 percent in Denmark). For staff in Denmark and England, a detailed account of their reply was recorded. Some staff, around the same proportion for each country, objected to the terms in which the question had been couched, problematizing the term 'advice'. But the ways in which they did so were different. Some of the staff in England seemed to take a more relativistic view point; for example one replied: '[We] can advise [them] if they ask, but we're not qualified to say what they should be doing'. and another: 'Not strictly, no. There is what's socially acceptable and what's not, but you can't live anyone's life'. Compared with their Danish counterparts, the English workers' responses seemed to have less professional security. The replies of pedagogues in Danish homes revealed greater confidence in their own values, and in their own relationships with the young people, for example:

> For me the examples are not that important, but the process [is]. It is important to follow up so that they feel remembered. We have talked about hash and [substance] abuse and about the physical con-sequences and the impact on schoolwork. I have said to a young person ... [Is] your life worth so little that you are [should be] allowed to do it [take drugs]? It is about presence, respect, it is the process that is important also in their lives.

> We can only move things [forward] together [i.e., with the child], and we can only do so when they believe in us, they dare listen to us and only then is what we say useful for them.

> Advice as such does not have a big effect. In dialogue, you make them think a little. It helps to be in dialogue. You tell what you think and they tell what they think. [It's important] that we give space for their understanding of reality. Advice in my opinion doesn't have a big effect, whereas to be in dialogue [about something] does.

Being in dialogue with a young person is typical of the 'reflexive' approach typical of social pedagogy. As discussed, it also relates to the attachment concept of 'mind-mindedness', which Howe (2005) argues is intrinsically therapeutic.

Key working: responsibilities

Another aspect of daily responsibilities for some residential pedagogues is to be a key worker. Key working is a frequently used system in group care, whereby staff are allocated one or more young people for whom they are particularly responsible. Key working can operate on various levels. It can be an administrative function, so that all paperwork, records and necessary procedures relating to one resident are maintained by one staff member. Key working can also be based mainly in the relationship between worker and child: the child knows that their key worker knows them, and can be turned to for support in everyday life. Or the key worker can combine both types of responsibilities. As we saw in Chapter 2, from what we had learned in the first study, the relationship model is an essential part of the pedagogic approach to working with children in residential care.

Table 5.1 shows that nearly two-thirds of informants were key workers for one or more young people, ranging from half of the English staff to 71–74 percent in Germany and Denmark. We also looked at the overall approach adopted by staff working with an individual child, (either when key working, or, in the minority of cases where the staff member was not a key worker, with the young person they knew best).

We asked staff the following questions, and probed to obtain full answers, about the child whom they knew best (mostly the child for whom they were key worker): 'What are your responsibilities in relation to that child? ... What is your role in working with him/her? ... What are you trying to achieve? We coded all their responses in terms of whether they described any of the following: employing a broadly therapeutic approach towards the young person; pedagogic responsibilities towards them (either mentioned as being pedagogically responsible or with more specific examples, such as working with the whole child, sharing their daily lives); providing emotional support; short-term behaviour management; procedural/organizational functions, and reference to long-term aims for child.

There were differences in the numbers of such roles and functions reported. For example, in Denmark, pedagogues reported more types of responsibility (2.7 on average) than staff in England or Germany. The types of responsibility reported also varied significantly between the countries (see Table 5.4). Staff in Denmark and Germany identified pedagogic responsibilities as the major component of their work (97 percent and 94 percent respectively).

Given that the pedagogic approach is not familiar in England, it is hardly surprising that staff in English residential homes did not respond in terms of pedagogy. So, because the pedagogic approach overlaps to some extent with (i) therapeutic approaches and (ii) providing emotional support, we collapsed these three categories into a new variable which we called 'relational' responsibilities. Table 5.4 shows the differences that emerged between the three countries: with respect to this new variable, staff in England were much less likely than their colleagues in Denmark or Germany to identify 'relational' approaches as part of their responsibilities as a key worker (40 percent of staff in England, 94 percent in Germany and 97 percent in Denmark).

Staff in Danish residential homes referred significantly more often to

Table 5.4: Types of approaches towards the young person for whom staff had key worker responsibilities (or knew best), by country, numbers and percentages

Type of approach	England N (%)	Germany N (%)	Denmark N (%)	Total N (%)
Procedural approach:**	29 (60)	2 (4)	2 (5)	33 (25)
Relational (pedagogic, therapeutic, and emotional):**	19 (40)	44 (94)	37 (97)	100 (75)
Short-term behaviour management:*	12 (25)	1 (2)	3 (8)	16 (12)
Reference to long-term aims:**	11 (23)	15 (32)	27 (71)	53 (40)
Other type of approach:†	9 (19)	5 (11)	11 (29)	25 (19)
Not known:†	0 (0)	1 (2)	0 (0)	1 (1)
Total number of cases:	48 (100)	47 (100)	38 (100)	133 (100)
Missing cases:	3 (–)	3 (–)	0 (–)	6 (–)

Notes: † Not significant; * $p<0.01$; ** $p<0.001$. A multiple response table: staff could have reported more than one approach to the way they work with young people. Therefore columns may not sum to 100%.

long-term aims for the child (mentioned by 71 percent in Denmark, compared to 23 percent in England and 32 percent in Germany) ($p<0.001$). In contrast, staff in England were more likely to report responsibilities for children's short-term behaviour management, (25 percent, compared to 2 percent for Germany and 8 percent for Denmark) ($p<0.005$). But overall, the focus of staff in England was more strongly on procedural or organizational responsibilities on behalf of young people: 60 percent of staff in English establishments reported these, compared to 4 percent of staff in Germany and 5 percent in Denmark ($p<0.001$).

In summary, ways of being a key worker differed across countries. A relational and a longer term approach defined the Danish and German methods of working with 'key' children, while the English approach was more focused on procedures and short-term behaviour management. Arguably, the difference between England and the other two countries may be accounted for in terms of the lack of a clearly defined and coherent professional education for residential staff in England; in the other two countries, this education focuses on the child's upbringing – their education in the broadest sense – and on the relationship between children and the staff. It involves (as we saw in Chapter 2) both the head and the heart. The qualification for residential care work in England is competency-based, and as such is focused on managing the 'here-and-now'. In the absence of the pedagogue's professional preparation, English workers put procedural responsibilities to the fore. Yet, compared with colleagues in Denmark and Germany, English staff were working in smaller establishments with higher staff-to-child ratios: settings where one might expect that personal relationships would be possible to achieve irrespective of training backgrounds and levels.

How did staff think about young people?

We also asked residential care workers to describe either their 'key child' or the child they knew best. The intention was to discover the extent to which the relational approach, associated with pedagogic training, was reflected in how staff replied.

Table 5.5: Staff description of young person for whom they were a key worker, or whom they knew best, in mainly personal and positive terms, or otherwise

	England N (%)	Germany N (%)	Denmark N (%)	Total N (%)
Personal and mainly positive:	18 (35)	15 (33)	25 (76)	58 (46)
Impersonal or mainly negative, or problem oriented:	33 (65)	27 (64)	8 (24)	68 (54)
Total:	51 (100)	42 (100)	33 (100)	126 (100)
Missing cases:	3 (–)	9 (–)	6 (–)	18 (–)

Note: *** p<0.001.

Responses were grouped for analysis according to the following two categories:

1   A personal and mainly positive account, for example:

> She's a typical teenager and you know what comes with that ... She's a lovely kid, very giving, generous, thoughtful. And then you see a completely different side of her when she's angry – vicious, nasty. When it explodes she explodes, so she's not nasty, it's a simmering pot. I don't think she knows how to express her feelings ... She feels trapped in the whole system, finds it confusing.
>
> (Member of staff in English establishment)

2   An impersonal, or mainly negative or problem oriented account, for example:

> He's a street child – street culture – very independent. Before coming here he was on the streets. He's not very academic, prefers hanging around with his friends, smoking weed. Petty crime committed, quite challenging. He doesn't integrate with the others here, sees them as little children – he has his own agenda. Today he's going to be tagged to make sure he observes his curfew ... I tend to get the challenging ones.
>
> (Member of staff in English establishment)

Table 5.5 shows that across all three countries, 46 percent (58) of staff gave a description that was mainly positive and focused on the young person rather than specifically upon their problems. However, in this table the pattern of responses is slightly altered from that reported earlier with respect to different approaches to key working. Notably, rather than workers in Denmark and Germany having a similar pattern, this time the German and English informants responded in similar ways. Workers in Denmark were more positively child oriented in their descriptions (76 percent compared with 33 percent in Germany and 35 percent of in England) and very few saw 'their' young people in terms of ease of management, or their personality or behavioural problems. These differences were statistically significant (p<0.001).

But what makes the pedagogues in Denmark so much less focused on problems and management and so much more focused on the positive strengths of an individual in residential care? This way of describing young people may reflect not just the pedagogic approach, which is characteristic of both Danish and German professional education, but also the relatively high level of training enjoyed by pedagogues in Denmark, which may provide a stronger theoretical basis for conceptualizing children in positive ways. Another, perhaps contributory, explanation may lie in more general cultural and social democratic traditions in Denmark which emphasize an inclusive, participatory society based on notions of citizenship and equality (see Chapter 1). This is an approach which encompasses children, as participants in the wider society (Jensen and Hansen 2003).

Responses to vignettes

We explored pedagogues' practice further, using a series of vignettes, or 'short stories about hypothetical characters in specified circumstances' (Finch 1987: 1). According to Finch, vignettes enable discussion of beliefs and norms in a situated way. In order to examine informants' practice – or at least what they would portray as their practice – we presented them with hypothetical situations and asked them, 'How would you react? What would you do?' These vignettes were used successfully in the first part of the study as triggers to start discussion (Boddy et al. 2003; Cameron 2004). Categories for the analysis of responses, described below, were derived from the earlier work. Informants quite frequently said they had had to deal with very similar situations in their daily work, so we were confident that the responses would accurately reflect norms of perceived 'good' practice.

As part of our comparisons of staff in England, Denmark and Germany we used three 'staged' vignettes. Each vignette comprised two or three parts,

presenting an escalation of a hypothetical situation. Across the three vignettes there were seven stages in total.

- (i) A girl, aged around 12 years, tells you that she is missing her
  parents. One night you find her crying in her room (ii) The same girl
  is two hours late coming back from a day out with her father. She
  phones and says she would like to stay the night with her father
  (although this is not in his access arrangements).
- (i) Two children do not get on at all well together; A says that he does
  not want to be near B at table (ii) Something we haven't told you
  before – A is a refugee; B has made insults about his dark skin colour
  (iii) One day you find them physically fighting.
- (i) One night you find a group of children drinking beer on the
  premises (ii) A few days later, late at night, you get a call from the
  police to say one of the children in this group is in the town centre,
  looking as if they might have taken drugs.

In order to clarify national differences an analysis was conducted across
the vignettes, summarizing ways of working according to the following
categories:

1 *'Action'* or answers that implied a decision to re-organize arrangements seen as contributing to the situation, including long-term
   plans regarding the child;
2 *'Collaboration'*, where the staff member said they would speak to
   other staff about the situation;
3 *'It depends'*, a more reflective response, when the staff member might
   outline different responses depending on specific circumstances;
4 *'Emotional'* support, which covered responses that implied immediate emotional support, physical contact and/or attempts to learn the
   child's perspective;
5 *'Fact seeking'* responses that sought other information from the child;
6 *'Procedural'* responses, covering any response in terms of regulations
   or procedures, including explaining rules or procedures to the child,
   reporting the situation to the manager or supervisor; and
7 *'External help sought'*, responses where the member of staff indicated
   that they would seek external help or advice, or that the child would
   be referred to an external agency.

The analysis was conducted in terms of type of response, within and
between countries, across all of the vignettes and their various stages. Table
5.6 presents the means for each type of response, in descending order of
magnitude.

Table 5.6: Staff responses to vignettes: mean (sd) number of responses in each category, summed across seven vignettes

Staff response	English Means (sd)	German Means (sd)	Danish Means (sd)	Total Means (sd)
Action:†	3.73 (1.50)	4.02 (1.44)	3.32 (1.07)	3.72 (1.39)
Procedural:***	3.49 (1.69)	1.84 (1.18)	3.58 (1.65)	
Emotional support:***	2.90 (1.19)	4.34 (1.40)	3.26 (1.01)	3.52 (1.37)
External support sought:***	1.51 (1.21)	0.54 (0.61)	0.37 (0.54)	0.85 (0.99)
It depends:***	1.27 (1.52)	2.08 (1.60)	4.66 (1.73)	2.49 (2.11)
Collaboration:***	0.73 (1.00)	0.76 (1.27)	2.18 (1.63)	1.14 (1.44)
Fact seeking:***	0.65 (0.93)	3.12 (1.62)	2.92 (1.73)	2.16 (1.84)

Notes: † Not significant; *** $p<0.001$.

For workers in England, an 'action' response was most frequent, followed by one that involved carrying out laid-down procedures, and, next most frequently, providing emotional support. They spoke of seeking further information about a situation much less frequently than staff in residential homes informed by the pedagogic tradition. For German workers, on the other hand, an emotional support response ranked highest, followed by, second, taking action, and, third, seeking other facts about the situation from the child. For staff in Denmark, 'it depends' responses ranked, as we have seen, highest, followed by reference to required procedures, and, third, taking action. Workers in Denmark spoke in terms of collaboration with colleagues more than other staff (mean=2.18, s.d=1.63; $p<0.001$); in England, informants referred to seeking 'external support' significantly more than their Danish and German colleagues (mean=1.51, s.d.=1.21; $p<0.001$).

The high use of 'it depends' (mean=4.66, s.d=1.73) demonstrates the Danish pedagogue engaging in a reflective mode, more than workers in either Germany or England, where 'it depends' did not figure in the top three responses at all, but ranked lower (for England in fifth place with a mean of 1.27 (s.d.=1.52), and for Germany in fourth place (mean=2.08, s.d.=1.60); (between country differences: $p<0.001$).

Barter and Renold (2000) have argued that vignettes encourage the response 'it depends' because they necessarily offer 'snapshots' of practice that demand further contextual information. In this case, the amount of information was equally available to informants in all three countries, but only staff in Denmark made extensive use of the 'it depends' code.

So it would appear that being reflective, considering alternative possibilities dependent on the circumstances is an important way of working for pedagogues in Denmark. Again, this may reflect their pedagogic education and training which encourages a contextualized response based on under-standings that staff and residents live in a dynamic and complex situation. However, it may reasonably be asked why, if pedagogic education and tra-ditions are equally prevalent in Denmark and Germany, the results for the two countries are so different and why German informants do not say 'it depends' as frequently as those in Denmark. If reflection is a central tenet of pedagogic training and the majority of staff in German residential care have a pedagogy qualification, then why are German responses so similar to that of England?

One main difference between the informants from Denmark and those from Germany is the level of the professional qualification held: as we saw in Chapter 4, pedagogues in Germany are more likely to hold a medium level qualification and less likely to hold a high level qualification than their col-leagues in Denmark. It may be that the ability to work with contingency that underlies 'it depends' responses is a feature of confidence and knowledge associated with higher level educational qualifications.

Discussion

The main theme of this chapter is that pedagogic education and training, based as it is in a coherent and consistent discipline, makes a difference to practice and to an understanding of practice possibilities in residential care. Moreover, the level of training undertaken makes a difference to practice.

While the broad picture of roles and responsibilities in residential care is similar across countries, there are important cross-national differences within our sample. In Germany, fewer staff worked with one group of children only, than in the other two countries. In England, fewer staff had key worker responsibilities than their counterparts in Germany and Denmark. In Eng-land, staff worked less often with parents; staff in Denmark were most likely to do so. In Denmark, staff had a wider range of key worker responsibilities than staff in Germany and England.

In offering emotional support to young people, workers in Denmark most frequently reported that they responded by listening to the young people, in England staff reported listening least frequently. Staff in Danish children's homes most frequently suggested alternative strategies for dealing with a difficult situation, while staff in German homes did so least frequently. There was more emphasis on combining empathic and discursive approaches for Danish, and to a lesser extent, German staff, while the English workers relied more heavily on discursive approaches, on talking and discussing rather than listening and empathizing.

Staff in England were much less likely to identify a relational approach towards the child whom they knew best, or for whom they were a key worker, than staff in Germany or Denmark. The parenting and attachment literature that we have discussed, would suggest that this is disadvantageous for young people. Instead, workers in England more frequently referred to procedural or organizational responsibilities and to short-term behavioural management than staff in the other countries, indicating a less personal professional role. Workers in Denmark showed a more long-term approach to their key worker roles than did the others, and described the children they worked with in positive and relational ways rather than negative or management-oriented ways.

In response to vignettes used to gauge normative responses to hypothetical situations, workers in Denmark reported more and more varied responses than other workers and, especially, much higher levels of reflective 'it depends' responses, although not to the exclusion of other responses. Taking action and providing emotional support responses dominated the English and German accounts in response to these hypothetical situations.

In some ways, 'it depends' may be seen as a characteristically Danish pedagogic response. Jensen and Hansen (2003), for example, found in a study of pedagogic work with young children in Danish childcare centres (where workers have the same basic training as residential care workers), that 'it depends' is a clear feature of pedagogic decision-making, and that negotiation and collaboration is a part of daily life and work in children's services, because values and actions are constantly debated:

> The pedagogical work cannot be organised or based on standards or plans. It is a condition of the work that there are no certain and objective answers and that it is impossible to follow strict plans. It is sometimes said about pedagogy that the answers are always subject to 'it depends on'. The concrete situation, the context, intentions, etc. always play a role and since the pedagogic culture is characterised by a tradition of democratic actions, the daily work will inevitably be marked by many discussions. Values and actions are continuously up for discussion.
>
> (Jensen and Hansen 2003: 152)

The pedagogic approach is interpreted in a distinctive way in contemporary Danish children's services: it may be similar, but it is not necessarily identical to that of other countries with pedagogic traditions. In Denmark, pedagogues are educated to have confidence in discussing many possibilities for courses of action, but also to take action, having considered those possibilities. In the findings, both on how emotional support is offered and on how workers respond to vignettes, a clear picture emerged of pedagogues in Denmark combining two elements of practice: a relational and reflective approach to work with young people *and* adhering to the structures and procedures in place in the establishment when taking action alongside, on behalf of and with the young person.

Overall, we have argued that the cross-national differences we have found are attributable not just to the pedagogic approach adopted, but also to levels and types of professional education. It may also be true that there are distinctive ways of practice that reside in professional cultures, nationally. What was remarkable in the results presented in this chapter was the degree of pedagogic coherence that was found in the responses to different questions among workers in Danish establishments. Responses to questions of orientations to practice in Germany and England indicated more variation, with German responses showing the influence of the pedagogic approach but less distinctively so than Danish responses.

Arguably, managing uncertainty requires professional confidence and knowledge. The question remains: how important is it to have workers who can work with uncertainty and at the same time maintain empathic, reflective and practical relationships with young people? If, as we hold, these are highly desirable characteristics, it is necessary to confront the necessity for high levels of training in order to achieve them. On the basis of evidence provided in this chapter, it seems that pedagogic training has much to offer. Higher levels of pedagogic qualification appear to be related to largely positive conceptualizations of children and young people, and pedagogic training promotes reflective professional practice, which in turn supports staff in 'listening' to young people, offering emotional support and taking action on their behalf.

6 A good start for young people?

Introduction

In considering the relative value of the English and continental European approaches to residential care work, the implications of these approaches for the young people who are looked after must be paramount. Put simply, is the pedagogic approach associated with better 'outcomes' for young people in residential care? This is an important question, because in England, and elsewhere in Europe, looked-after young people in public care are among the most vulnerable in society, showing evidence of disadvantage in terms of a number of indicators. As we noted in Chapter 1, looked-after young people have higher rates of teenage pregnancy than those to be found in the rest of the population, they are less likely to be in education or employment than others, and a higher proportion of them are recorded as having engaged in criminal activity (e.g., SEU 2003).

The study described in this section did not research long-term outcomes for young people. We did not follow the young people interviewed through into independent adult life, looking at possible indicators of social inclusion/exclusion. We looked instead at aspects of the young people's life in their current establishments that were likely to be associated with favourable life chances. The current understanding of the English government is that for many looked after children, poor experiences of education and care contribute to later social exclusion, and that there are five key reasons for this:

1. Too many young people's lives are characterized by instability;
2. Young people in care spend too much time out of school or any other place of learning;
3. Children do not have sufficient help with their education if they get behind;
4. Carers are not expected, or equipped, to provide sufficient support and encouragement at home for learning and development; and
5. Children in care need more help with their emotional, mental or physical health and wellbeing.

(SEU 2003: 11, 12)

In this chapter, we examine some facets (described below) of these 'key reasons' in relation to different national policy and practice approaches.

Different populations, different outcomes?

One difficulty in addressing questions of outcomes relates to differences in the populations of young people looked after. In discussing the results that follow, it is important to bear in mind that, as noted in previous chapters, the populations of young people looked after differ across the countries (see Table 3.1). A far smaller proportion of children and young people are in public care, and in particular in residential care, in England than elsewhere.

Given these differences, young people in residential care in England could thus be said to be at the 'extreme' end of the looked-after population – often those for whom other forms of provision have been unsuccessful. Our analysis of public policy for young people looked after (see Chapter 1) also indicated that residential care is understood differently in Denmark and Germany where, compared to England, residential accommodation is more likely to be seen as a positive placement option for children and young people than as something of a last resort, for example compared to foster care. With an emphasis on pedagogy, or 'education in the broadest sense', a placement may be made for broadly educative, rather than more narrowly protective, reasons. To adopt the language of current English policy (e.g., Department for Education and Skills 2003; Department of Health 2004), the pedagogic emphasis on promoting the child's potential for development means that the placement must do more than just 'safeguard' the child.

Given such differences in resident populations and in placement policy, we could predict that English young people are likely to appear disadvantaged relative to their counterparts elsewhere in Europe, for example on outcomes such as school attendance. But what underlies this disadvantage? It is entirely plausible that the more disadvantaged the child and the more their background is one of relative social exclusion, the more likely it is that they are disaffected from schooling, one of the dominant social institutions of childhood.

In other words, if disadvantage resides more in the English population of looked-after children than in Denmark or Germany, any cross-country differences as to outcomes could be explained by the characteristics of young people on entering residential care; such differences would be less dependent on other aspects of policy and practice such as the pedagogic approach. This chapter will present analyses that address this issue.

There is, however, a further question, one which arises around staffing. If English young people are reported to have higher levels of difficulty in terms of key outcome indicators, we need to consider how these indicators relate to the workforce issues discussed earlier in this volume. If English residential homes are populated with young people particularly vulnerable to disadvantage, how does this relate to the variations we have documented in staff qualifications and practice?

Our earlier analysis indicates that English residential staff were less well equipped – in terms of professional knowledge and training – to meet the challenges posed by the young people in their care than their continental counterparts. The English workforce we studied was characterized by less stability and lower levels of formal qualifications and in-service training than staff in Denmark or Germany. At the same time England, as we shall see, had the highest staff to child ratios of the three countries. England, Germany and Denmark also appeared to differ in relation to interview questions about working practices, and staff conceptions of the work and of the children in their care. This variation could be seen in relation to their perception of the responsibilities involved in their job, their accounts of children, and their responses to vignettes about hypothetical situations involving young people. How do these cross-country differences relate to children's life chances? In attempting to answer that question, this chapter will consider how workforce characteristics, and aspects of staff practice and conceptions of the work relate to child outcome indicators.

Sources of data

The analyses presented in this chapter draw on quantitative data from interviews with young people, staff and managers of residential homes in all three countries[1]. Establishment managers were asked about the characteristics of young people currently resident including the ethnicity of the young people living in the home and the nature of placements: how many were voluntary placements to which parents had given their consent; how many had been put in place as the result of a care order; and for how many had the young person's criminal behaviour been involved in the decision to place them in care. Heads were also asked about the distance of the residential establishment from the family homes of the young people; how many young people had special needs or disabilities; their use of health, community and education services and their engagement in the community.

Heads were asked to provide summary data from records of young people resident during 2001 about a range of 'outcome' indicators. Given the study's concern with risk of social exclusion, managers were asked to report the proportion of young people aged under and over 16 who were in education, those aged 16 and over who were in employment, and those who were in neither education nor employment. Lack of stability in care is also thought to be a risk factor for social exclusion (SEU 2003): as an indicator of placement stability in each residential establishment, managers reported the rate of turnover of young people in the home during 2001, and the average placement duration. According to the Social Exclusion Unit (2003) English young people looked after in public care are two and a half times more likely to be teenage parents relative to the general population, and so managers were also asked to report the number of pregnancies among young women under 19 years of age who were resident during 2001. Anti-social or criminal behaviour may be an indicator of social exclusion, and so managers reported the number of criminal offences by residents recorded for 2001.

In this chapter, these broader data will be supplemented by evidence from interviews with the young people themselves concerning their education and use of health and community services. A fuller account of young people's perspectives on their everyday lives in residential care will be provided in the next chapter.

Analytic strategy

The cross-sectional research described in this volume does not permit causal analysis. However, it is possible to consider the extent to which staff and establishment characteristics, and working practices (including facets of the pedagogic approach, but also broader variables such as staff ratios and levels of qualification), are associated with any variations in the outcome indicators with which we are concerned, including those relating to young people's use of health services, education, employment, rates of criminal offences and community engagement.

Initially, cross-country differences in key outcome indicators from head and young people data were investigated using comparative statistical methods: analysis of variance and cross-tabulation (chi-square analysis) as appropriate. Subsequently, these correlational analyses were followed by linear regression to identify variables other than country that accounted for variance in the outcome indicators of interest.[2]

In the analyses carried out for this chapter, we looked at links between outcome variables such as the percentage of young people aged 16 and over who were not in education or employment and the following: the percentage of young people with voluntary, court ordered or juvenile offence related placements; the percentage placed within their local authority; resident turnover in 2001; the total number of young people on one site; staff to child ratios; whether the provider was a local authority, a private commercial company or a private non profit-making organization; the number of children's and family support services provided on site; difficulties reported by the head about staff recruitment or retention; policies about young people's well-being and progress at school; policies about employment. From staff interviews the following variables were included: the member of staff's salary; their years in employment in the establishment; strategies for providing emotional support to young people; responsibilities in relation to the child for whom they were the key worker, and their description of this child; and responses to vignettes about hypothetical situations involving young people.

Those variables that were significantly correlated with outcome indicators were included in stepwise linear regression, with country entered on the first step, and all other variables entered together on the second step. For simplicity, any variables that did not make a statistically significant contribution to the statistical model were then excluded, so the results presented here report only on the best models accounting for variance in outcome indicators.

Characteristics of residential homes

The cross-country differences in policies for young people's residential care were reflected in the characteristics of homes visited during the research. Of the 24 English homes with information on provider type, the largest proportion (14) was in the private sector; most – but not all – were for-profit organizations, unaffiliated to any religious organization. Nine of the English units were public sector local authority homes and one was a secure unit. In Germany, data on provider type were available for ten establishments. Three of these were state sector units, four belonged to religious non-profit, and three to secular, non-profit providers. In Denmark, half of the 12 establishments visited were state provided, five belonged to secular non-profit and one to a religious non-profit organization. The countries differed in the size of establishments, both in terms of the number of units on site (most English homes were single unit establishments, with much more variation in Denmark and Germany) and the number of staff and young people resident (see Table 6.1). English residential units were significantly smaller than those in Denmark and Germany, and less likely to accommodate children aged below 12 or over 15 years: these findings are perhaps not surprising given the English policy preference for foster care, especially for younger children, and a move in this country towards smaller residential units than in previous years. English homes were also smaller in terms of staff numbers; however, the ratio of staff to young people in England was significantly higher than in Denmark or in Germany.

At the same time, there was significantly higher turnover of young people in England than elsewhere – almost twice the rate reported in Germany – a difference that perhaps reflects the English conception of residential care as a final resort or emergency option, rather than a positive long-term choice for residential care. This difference may also reflect the fact that at least two of the English homes visited were emergency units, where placements were supposed to be limited to three months duration (although longer placements were reported on these sites). However, the resident turnover in these 'short-term' establishments was not significantly higher than those in the rest of the English sample.

Table 6.1: Characteristics of residential homes visited, as reported by home managers: mean N (sd)

	England (23 homes)	Germany (18 homes)	Denmark (12 homes)
Units in establishment:[1]***	2.3 (4.8)	11.3 (10.9)	3.5 (1.5)
Young people			
Total young people in unit:**	6.3 (3.4)	23.3 (28.5)	21.2 (9.1)
Aged 11 years or younger:**	0.13 (0.63)	5.9 (8.2)	5.7 (6.2)
Aged 12 to 15 years:†	4.7 (2.5)	8.7 (12.2)	9.9 (7.8)
Aged 16 and over:**	1.4 (2.1)	8.7 (10.0)	5.6 (7.7)
% of young people staying on-site at weekend:**	86.7 (32.5)	75.2 (29.1)	52.1 (24.7)
Rate of resident turnover in 2001:**	0.65 (0.36)	0.32 (0.31)	0.41 (0.20)
Staff			
Total residential social workers/ pedagogues:†	11.3 (4.0)	26.1 (35.6)	26.2 (10.4)
Total of all direct care staff:[2]**	20.8 (13.4)	45.0 (52.5)	51.2 (27.3)
Staff:child ratio (all direct care staff to young people in unit):**	3.7 (1.9)	2.1 (1.4)	2.5 (0.8)

Notes: 1 These are the number of individual homes that come under one management per establishment. 2 Direct care staff were defined as all those with direct involvement and caring responsibilities for young people, to allow for potential variations in roles and responsibilities across countries. Thus, this category included, for example, teaching and nursing staff who worked directly with young people on site.
† Not significant; * $p<0.05$; ** $p<0.01$; *** $p<0.001$.

Characteristics of current residents

Managers' reports

Table 6.2 summarizes some key characteristics of young people currently resident in the establishments participating in the study, as reported by managers. In each country, a similar proportion of residents (around 90 percent) were reported to be nationals of that country, and there were no differences between countries in the reported proportion of residents with learning difficulties, or sensory or physical disabilities. The average percentage of young people with learning difficulties appears higher in Germany, but this was not statistically significant and in fact there was a great deal of variation across homes in all three countries.

Table 6.2: Cross-country variation in young people's characteristics, reported by home managers: mean percentage (sd)

	England	Germany	Denmark
Country nationals†	92.3 (16.6)	92.3 (8.5)	89.2 (11.8)
Placed within local authority*	48.9 (44.1)	72.3 (34.8)	88.3 (26.5)
Young people with disabilities			
Learning difficulties†	15.5 (26.6)	24.4 (22.6)	6.8 (9.2)
Sensory disabilities†	1.0 (5.0)	2.9 (4.7)	0.52 (1.2)
Physical disabilities†	1.8 (6.3)	1.9 (2.75)	0.50 (1.2)
Placement type			
Voluntary***	45.9 (27.9)	80.7 (27.6)	85.0 (13.9)
Court ordered***	42.9 (30.8)	15.8 (26.5)	9.5 (11.8)
Related to criminal offence†	13.1 (19.0)	3.8 (4.5)	5.5 (11.6)

Notes: † Not significant; * $p<0.05$; ** $p<0.01$; *** $p<0.001$.

Clear cross-country differences were apparent, however, in the proportion of young people with voluntary placements, as would be expected given the policy differences outlined earlier in this volume. Young people in Denmark and Germany were significantly more likely to be placed by voluntary agreement with their parents, and English young people were more likely to be placed by court order. This finding may be seen as lending weight to the hypothesis that the English residents were more disadvantaged and perhaps had a more troubled history than the others.

In all three countries, it is policy that placements for young people should be made as close to their family home as possible. In continental Europe, this reflects the pedagogic concern with the young person's social networks and what in German is termed the *Lebenswelt* (their 'living world' or their everyday life). In Germany, where the majority of looked-after young people are in residential care, policies based on the need for individualized care planning around the young person's *Lebenswelt* have led to a diversification of placement possibilities. German state and federal policies support the establishment of small local facilities, and of different forms of residential provision such as 'five day settings' (where young people return to their families of origin at the weekend). However, this practice was not confined to such establishments, in any of the countries studied. Half of young people in Danish establishments were reported to stay on-site at weekends, compared with three-quarters of German young people, and 85 percent of English residents.

Importantly, in Denmark and Germany, residential care is usually conceptualized as a positive placement choice for young people, an opportunity for therapeutic and developmental intervention, rather than as a final option when other possibilities are exhausted. English policy preference for foster care rather than residential placement has meant a decline in the number of children's homes in some areas, and this may make it more difficult for young people to be placed close to home. These policies appear to have been reflected in the countries' relative success at local placement; young people in England were significantly less likely than those in Denmark or Germany to have been placed within their local authority.

Contact with families

As might be expected given the above findings, though not statistically significant, fewer English young people (74.6 percent; sd 29.0) were in contact with their families than was the case in Germany (92.7 percent; sd 22.1) or Denmark (90.9 percent; sd 13.8; p<0.07). This report from managers was borne out by data from staff interviewed. According to staff, almost half of young people in Denmark (mean 47.4 percent; sd=19.4) and in Germany (44.1 percent; sd=17.0) had seen a member of their family in the last month, compared to just under a third in England (32.2 percent; sd=25.2; p<0.001). Less pronounced – albeit statistically significant – variation was evident in staff accounts of the numbers of young people who had visits from family in the last week (perhaps because this was relatively unusual in all three countries).

There are probably several reasons for the lower levels of contact that young people in England had with family members. Not least, a higher proportion in England had court ordered placements, and one might expect that the family difficulties that lead to a care order would mitigate against maintenance of contact between the child and other family members. While interviewees in all countries spoke of the challenges of working with young people's families, the pedagogue's education and approach to work with the child emphasizes family members' position in the child's network of relationships, and in Denmark and Germany, family members usually continue to have responsibility and involvement in decision-making about the child, even when a care order is in place.

In order to ascertain the sorts of issues that managers themselves thought were important, we asked them about any particular concerns they had for young people's welfare. While there were no statistically significant differences across countries in the areas of concern mentioned, it is noteworthy that almost half of English respondents (11/25) highlighted problems relating to other professional agencies, compared with a third (4/12) of heads of establishment in Germany and just one out of 11 in Denmark. Four managers in England expressed criticisms of social services departments, either at the level of practice or in relation to lack of provision in the local area. Two mentioned communication difficulties with social workers 'not working together', and one manager tied this to the low status of residential care work.

These comments echo the points raised in discussions of workforce issues earlier in this volume, providing an indication of how such issues are seen by managers as linked to young people's welfare. That heads of establishments in England should respond in this way is challenging, given the public policy emphasis on multiagency collaboration, especially when it comes to work with children (e.g., DfES 2003; Department of Health 2004).

Young people interviewed

In total, 302 young people were interviewed across all three countries: 100 in England, 116 in Germany and 86 in Denmark.

There were no cross-country differences in the gender of young people who took part in interviews: in England 44.8 percent were female, compared with 43.1 percent in Germany and 38.4 percent in Denmark. In all countries, the young people ranged in age from 11 to 18 years (average: England 14.5 years; Germany 15.1 years; Denmark 14.7 years).

Of the 118 young people who provided information about their citizenship, a similar proportion to that reported by heads of establishment for all residents were country nationals (89.1 percent in England, 41/46 respondents; 92.5 percent in Germany, 37/40 young people; 90.6 percent or 29/32 Danish respondents). Ethnicity is classified differently in Germany and Denmark, and so direct intercountry comparisons were not possible on this variable. That said, there was some evidence of cross-country variation. Out of 95 English young people who defined their ethnicity, the most common groups were white British (69 young people, 73 percent) and black or black British (19 respondents; 20 percent). Two-thirds of Danish young people (57 out of 84) reported having two Danish parents and 32.1 percent (27 young people) described other ethnic origins, including mixed Danish and other parentage. In Germany, 115 young people provided information about their country of origin, of whom 105 (91.3 percent) were German; the most common other group was Turkish (three young people).

Placement stability also appeared to vary between countries, according to information provided by young people interviewed. Young people interviewed in England had been resident for on average 11.1 months (sd 19.5), compared to 30.9 months in Germany (sd 36.0) and 24.7 months in Denmark (sd 21.4).

These results did not appear to have been biased by inclusion in the analysis of two English homes designated as emergency/short stay provision. Repetition of the comparison excluding these two cases yielded equivalent results, which was unsurprising, given how recently many English respondents had moved into their establishment. The most common (modal) length of stay among respondents in England (13/99) was just three months; half the English sample had been in their current placement for six months or less, and only 30 percent for 12 months or more. These findings carry strong echoes of the Social Exclusion Unit's (2003) observation that the lives of too many young people in residential care in England are characterized by instability.

Education and employment

Managers' reports

Data on young people aged under 16 years who were not attending school were provided by 25 English, 11 German and 11 Danish heads of establishment. According to these data, 11.6 percent of English under 16-year-olds were not attending school at the time of the interview (sd=20.0), compared with 2.2 percent of German residents (sd=4.4) and only 1.6 percent of Danish residents in this age group (sd=4.5). This difference just failed to reach statistical significance (p<0.10).

Correlational analyses revealed a number of associations between the percentage of residents aged less than 16 years who were not attending school and a number of staff and head of establishment variables. However, most did not reach statistical significance and regression showed that only two were independent of country in explaining significant variance in the proportion of under 16-year-olds who were not attending school: the percentage of staff with no qualifications (r=0.33), and the number of years that staff interviewed had worked in the establishment (r=−0.41). Together, these variables explained 20 percent of the variance in the proportion of under 16-year-olds who were out of education (adjusted R^2=0.20; p<0.005).

A similar pattern was reported among young people aged 16 and over. In this age group, over half of English young people (54.9 percent; sd=79.3) were not in education or employment, compared with around a quarter of German teenagers (23.4 percent; sd=27.8) and only 5.2 percent (sd=7.7) of Danish young people. These data were provided by 16 English, 11 German and 11 Danish managers. Given these small numbers, it is perhaps not surprising that the apparent intergroup differences are not statistically significant (p<0.7). Nevertheless, the high proportion of English young people in this category is consistent with previous research on outcomes for looked-after young people (e.g., Meltzer et al. 2003) and is clearly a cause for concern.

Regression analyses indicated that, while other variables showed some degree of association with the percentage of young people aged 16 and over who were out of education and employment, only staff to child ratios (and not country) statistically predicted this outcome indicator. When this variable was included in stepwise regression, country ceased to account for significant variance in the outcome. Specifically, a higher staff to child ratio was associated with a higher percentage of residents aged 16 and over who were not in education or employment (adjusted R^2=0.15; $p \leq 0.01$).

Once again, this finding does not establish causality. Indeed it may be that a higher staff to child ratio is necessary in institutions where a greater proportion of residents are out of employment or education. However, such evidence undermines the contention that a high staff to child ratio is, of itself, protective against poor outcomes.

The education of young people interviewed

More detailed information about engagement with education was available from the young people whom we interviewed (summarized in Table 6.3). While every effort was made to seek consent for interview from all residents, it must be recognized that these data only represent a proportion of young people living in the establishments visited.

In considering the relative proportions of young people in education and in mainstream school we need to recognize that there may be contextual differences across countries. In England at least, non-attendance of school can be a factor in the breakdown of foster placements and the subsequent entry of children into residential care. At the same time, cross-country variations in the proportion of young people in education might reflect differences in provision of on-site educational services. Almost half of Danish establishments (5/11) provided education for residents, compared with a quarter of those in Germany (3/12) and one in five English homes (5/24, difference not significant). Similarly, Danish homes were more likely to employ teachers than those in England or Germany (p<0.005). Danish managers reported an average of three teaching posts per establishment (ranging from 0 to 11 in the 12 homes visited), compared with an average of 0.5 in Germany and England (English range 0–7.5 across 23 homes; 0–3 for the 17 German homes).

As might be expected given these figures, Table 6.3 shows that almost all German 12–14-year-olds were in mainstream school, compared with less than half of English young people and under a third in Denmark. In this age group, on-site schooling was the most common form of provision for Danish young people, used by almost two-thirds of those interviewed (24/39), compared with 12 out of 48 English young people, and only one out of 41 German respondents.

Intercountry differences were even more pronounced among young people aged 15–18. In this older age group, only one Danish respondent was not in education, compared with nearly a quarter of English interviewees and about one in six German respondents. At the same time, English young people were the least likely to be in mainstream school (only one in five, compared with over half in Denmark and Germany). The largest proportion

Table 6.3:   Engagement in education among young people interviewed

	England N (%)	Germany N (%)	Denmark N (%)	Total N (%)
*12–14-year-olds**				
Mainstream school:	17 (35)	35 (83)	11 (28)	63 (49)
On-site school:	12 (25)	1 (2)	24 (62)	37 (29)
Other: special school, tutor, other support, no education:	19 (37)	6 (14)	4 (10)	29 (22)
Total:	48 (100)	42 (100)	39 (100)	129 (100)
*15–18-year-olds**				
Mainstream school:	9 (18)	46 (62)	25 (53)	80 (47)
On-site school:	15 (29)	3 (4)	11 (23)	29 (17)
College or university:	6 (11.8)	5 (6.8)	4 (8.5)	15 (9)
Other: special school, tutor, other support:	9 (18)	8 (11)	6 (13)	18 (10)
No education:	12 (24)	12 (16)	1 (2)	25 (15)
Total:	51 (100)	74 (100)	47 (100)	172 (100)

Notes: * $p < 0.001$.

of young people interviewed in England (nearly a third) were educated at schools belonging to the residential care provider (usually on-site). This latter form of provision was used by a quarter of Danish young people in the older age group but by only three (out of 74) young people in Germany.

A somewhat different picture was apparent when young people aged 15–18 years were asked whether they had taken any public examinations in the last two years. Around half of English (22/46) and Danish (26/47) respondents said they had taken public examinations in this period; this compares with just over a third (25/72) German respondents ($p < 0.08$, ns). Furthermore, English interviewees reported having taken a larger number of public examinations in the last two years (average 1.3, range 0–8) than respondents in either Denmark (average 0.66, range 0–3) or Germany (0.38, range 0–2) ($p < 0.001$).

Looking more closely at the picture in England, of the 22 young people who had taken public examinations, six reported having sat an exam for a certificate of achievement, whereas 14 had taken at least one GCSE (mode = 1, maximum = 8). A small number reported other forms of assessment, such as SATS, college entry or adult literacy tests, but none reported taking A or AS levels, or any other higher level examinations.

Differences in the number of examinations taken may reflect cross-national variation in education and examining systems. For example, according to Eurydice/Eurostat (2005), fewer than 4 percent of Danish pupils attend schools where assessment at age 15 is used to determine progression to the next year of study, compared with over 95 percent in Germany and 60 percent in the UK. Similarly, practice for assessment at the end of general lower secondary education varies across German *Länder*: in most the final grade is set by the school's teachers, although in some cases – as happens in Denmark – the teachers' grading is externally verified. The English system – with externally set and graded examinations – is quite different, and this may account at least in part for the differences in our sample.

Contextual differences aside, country was not the only factor to account for variation in the number of examinations taken by 15–18-year-olds in our sample. Regression analyses indicated three variables (including country) that accounted for significant variation in reports of numbers of examinations taken: young people who reported sitting higher numbers of examinations lived in establishments whose managers had significantly more policies about higher education and where staff described more responsibilities in relation to the children in their care (adjusted R^2 = 0.16, p<0.001). Because there was more variation in the number of public examinations taken in the English sample than in Denmark or Germany, regression analysis was also conducted for England separately. The only variable to explain significant variance was staff report of the number of young people in the establishment who had visits from family within the last week (r=0.337; adjusted R^2=0.089; p<0.05), such that young people reported taking more examinations in establishments where a higher proportion of residents had received visits from family. While interesting, one can only speculate on possible reasons for this association. These may include population differences (for example, both family visits and taking examinations may be more common in establishments where residents come from less disadvantaged backgrounds, or show less challenging behaviour).

Alternatively, the association could reflect some aspect of the ethos of the care establishment, in supporting family contact and young people's education, or it may be that where family contact is functioning well (as seems likely if residents have had visits in the last week), it is protective against disadvantage in other areas. In fact, all these explanations are plausible and all are likely to be at least partly true. That said, it is important to recognize that a minority of young people in England (and in the other countries) had family visits in the last week, and so whatever the association, it does not apply to most looked-after young people. This last point is reflected in the observation that over 90 percent of the variance in examinations taken by English young people remained unexplained.

Employment of young people interviewed

Young people aged 16–18 who do not participate in education, training or employment are at risk of disadvantage in later life, for example in relation to later unemployment, poor health, drug use, depression and criminal activity (SEU 1999). Employment in this age group may offer experience, income and – perhaps particularly important for those in residential care – an opportunity to engage constructively with the wider community. Interviews with young people aged 15 and older included questions about employment, and showed clear cross-country differences in this respect. Only two of the 50 English respondents who answered these questions were in any kind of employment. Of these, one – a 16-year-old girl – did paid work helping look after animals at the on-site school she attended; the other – a 17-year-old boy – was no longer in education but had four Grade G GCSEs[3], and did paid work mending equipment in a local youth organization. While the majority of older young people interviewed in Denmark and Germany were not working, employment was nevertheless more common among respondents in these countries than in England (p<0.001).

In Germany, around a third of young people were engaged in some form of work: four (out of 74) did voluntary work and nine did other work or work experience, while another nine had paid employment (9/74). One young person worked in a lawyers' office and another for an architect, but more commonly mentioned forms of employment or work experience included work in supermarkets, in the building trade and in the catering trade. For example, one 16-year-old boy described paid work 'selling sausages and beer at the neighbouring sports club, cleaning the club house or the toilets', and another 17-year-old boy was doing work experience as a bricklayer. Similar work settings were described by Danish respondents of whom almost one-third (13/46) was in paid employment, and three described work experience. Young people worked in supermarkets and in manual labour including furniture removal, gardening and farming. One 18-year-old girl had previously done work experience as a pedagogical assistant, working for a child with physical disabilities.

Looking at how these employment figures relate to engagement in education, in England a third of young people interviewed (16/49) were neither in education nor employment, compared with a tenth of the sample in Germany and Denmark. While the small numbers involved do not permit statistical comparison, it is also noteworthy that in these countries most of those who were engaged in work or work experience were still in education too. Only three of the 23 respondents who were working in Germany were out of education, and in Denmark five out of 16 working young people were not in education at the time.

While some of the jobs described – as illustrated above – could provide work experience relevant to possible future careers, several young people described the sort of 'pocket money' jobs that connote 'ordinary' teenage life, such as 'washing pedagogues' cars for 5 Euros a car' (16-year-old German boy), 'delivering newspapers' (15-year-old German boy; 16-year-old Danish boy), or 'babysitting' (15-year-old German girl).

The balance of education and employment for young people was summed up well in the comments of one Danish manager:

> If they have wishes and they can cope then we find something. One child works in the kitchen, some work with the caretaker. A few [work] outside [the establishment], but the school, and to attend it, is the most important work for them.

An 18-year-old German girl, who was studying at a theatre school and had done acting work, joked that her establishment put pressure on residents to work, saying, '[It's] forced labour – if I wouldn't work here, I might not live here. One must make something here. But I also want [to work]. It isn't really forced labour'. Joking aside, the relatively high proportion of respondents in education and employment in Denmark and Germany is perhaps indicative of the success of these establishments and their staff, in encouraging and supporting young people's participation in the wider society. The manager of this young woman's establishment described a clear strategy for combining work and training opportunities, making use of contacts with companies and highlighting a role for employment as an 'accompaniment to vocational training', while acknowledging the difficulties of 'unsatisfying vocational opportunities, [with] training often beyond their capabilities'.

Such findings are clearly highly relevant to current English policy concerns about risk for social exclusion among young people in residential care; at the same time, these interviewees' comments provide a practical illustration of the pedagogic emphasis on promoting and supporting young people's development, in its broadest sense.

The health of young people

Managers' report of young people's use of health services

Difficulties in accessing health services is one of the 'key reasons' given by the Social Exclusion Unit (2003: 12) for young people underachieving in education and their subsequent disadvantage. According to this report, problems in accessing health services are intertwined with placement instability and are perhaps symptomatic of a wider dislocation from society among young people in residential care. To illuminate such concerns, managers were asked about difficulties with young people's use of health services.

More than three-quarters of English managers (19/24) reported problems in this area, compared with just over half of German respondents (7/12) and no Danish managers (p<0.001). Two-thirds of English managers attributed difficulties to young people's unwillingness to use health services (13 out of 20 respondents). The source of difficulty most commonly cited by German managers was that health services were unsupportive of young people's needs (mentioned by four out of seven). Two English and two German respondents highlighted cost issues, for example relating to payment for tests and specialist services.

German managers were less likely than those in England or Denmark to report regular health checks on children in their care in relation to developmental tests (p<0.10) and eye tests (p<0.05). In both cases, around half of German establishments had regular tests, compared with three-quarters or more of English and Danish homes. A similar pattern was apparent for hearing tests, but this did not reach statistical significance. In all countries, routine assessment by psychologists (either on entry or regularly throughout the young person's residency) was reported in less than a quarter of cases, and there were no cross-country differences.

Denmark was the only country in which all managers reported that all young people were registered with a local GP, but this did not differ statistically from Germany (10/12) or England (22/25). Similarly, there was no between country variation in the frequency of visits by a GP. English managers, however, were more likely to report regular visits by a nurse (p<0.005). Of the 11 (out of 25) English homes reporting regular nurse visits, eight reported that the nurse attended at least once a month. No German managers and only one in Denmark reported regular nurse visits (in this case, the visit had occurred in the last nine to 12 months). This cross-country difference cannot be fully explained by the presence of nurses on staff in the other countries; only three German homes, and none in Denmark, employed nursing staff. However, in England visits by a nurse is stipulated in legislation for looked-after young people and so it is arguably surprising that regular nurse visits were not more widely reported in this country.

Pregnancies among young people under 19 years

In England, young people in care are two and a half times more likely to become teenage parents than those in the general population. Teenage pregnancy is in itself associated with a range of health risks, and if a child is born, relates to long-term disadvantage (SEU 1999).

Managers used establishment records from 2001 to report pregnancies among residents aged less than 19 years. English managers reported almost three times the rate of pregnancy (11.6 percent; sd=13.3) of those in Denmark (3.1 percent; sd=4.4), and more than twice that reported by German managers (4.6 percent; sd=5.9) (p<0.05).

England has the highest rate of teenage pregnancy in Western Europe (SEU 1999), so perhaps this finding is not surprising. What was striking, however, was that further analysis showed that staff characteristics played a more important role than country in explaining variation in pregnancy rates.

Lower rates of pregnancies among under 19-year-olds were reported in institutions where staff interviewed had higher rates of in-service training (r=−0.41), offered more fact-seeking responses to hypothetical dilemmas involving young people (r=−0.42), and intended to carry on in their current post for longer (r=−0.35), and when these three factors were taken into account, country no longer explained significant variance in the incidence of pregnancy. Instead, these three staff characteristics together accounted for nearly 30 percent of the variation in reported rates of pregnancies under 19 (adjusted R^2=0.284; p<0.005).

Variables that described the population of looked-after young people – such as the proportion with voluntary placements, those placed within the local authority, or those out of education – differed across country, but they did not predict variation in rates of pregnancy. In the present sample, we may conclude that cross-country differences in the care population did not account for risk of teenage pregnancy; staff characteristics did.

Young people's report of health service use

Young people interviewed were also asked about health appointments in the last year. As noted previously, difficulty accessing health services has been reported previously among young people in care in England and is perhaps indicative of a more general lack of engagement with community services in this population (SEU 2003).

There were no cross-country differences in reported attendance of appointments with doctors or dentists, although English young people were significantly more likely to have visited an optician (72/98, or 73.5 percent) than those in Denmark (25/85, or 29.4 percent) or Germany (38/116, or 32.8 percent; p<0.001).

German young people reported a higher proportion of health care appointments that were coded as 'other' (70/115 or 60.9 percent in Germany; 20/85 or 23.5 percent in Denmark; 15/98 or 15.3 percent in England; p<0.001). Not surprisingly, the nature of these 'other' health appointments varied considerably, including medical specialties such as cardiology, dermatology and eye specialists. Appointments with child and adolescent psychologists and psychiatrists were reported by 13 German respondents, but the category most commonly mentioned (by 18 out of 50 young women in the German sample) was gynaecology. Forms of service provision differ across countries, and so direct comparison would be ill-advised (for example, English young people may be accessing sexual health advice and services through visits to their general practitioner). That said, this pattern of service use bears consideration, in light of cross-country differences in rates of pregnancy among residents under 19 years of age.

Criminal offences

English policy concern about social exclusion for young people in care (SEU 1999, 2003) highlights the issue of criminal offending. According to the Social Exclusion Unit (2003), around one-quarter of adults in prison have spent time in care as children, and young people aged 16–18 who are out of education, training and employment (among whom those in residential care are disproportionately represented) are at higher risk of criminal activity. Criminal behaviour may also be a factor in foster placement breakdown, in England at least, and a reason for placement in residential care.

For some of the residents of the establishments we studied, juvenile offending had been a contributing factor in the events leading to a placement being made. It was more commonly reported as a contributing factor in English placements, although this did not reach statistical significance (see Table 6.2).

Heads of establishment were asked to report the number of criminal offences committed by young people resident during the year 2001. This figure was divided by the number of residents in 2001, to provide an index of the rate of offences per resident. In England, this figure was 1.73 offences per resident, compared with 0.092 in Germany and 0.158 in Denmark. While striking, this finding just failed to reach statistical significance ($p<0.06$).

Correlational analyses were again conducted to identify factors associated with variation in reported rates of offending. As with analyses of rates of pregnancy, characteristics of the care population – including the proportion of residents with offending as a contributory factor to placement – did not account for significant variation in rates of criminal offence. One-quarter of the variance in rates of offending (adjusted $R^2=0.265$; $p<0.001$) was explained by just two variables: staff to child ratio and staff reference to external sources of support in response to vignette situations.

Although staff to child ratio and vignette responses all varied across the three countries, country did not explain variance in offending when these two factors were taken into account. As previously, a higher staff to child ratio corresponded to poorer child outcomes – in this case, to higher rates of offending (r=0.40). At the same time, higher rates of offending were reported in institutions where staff were more likely to refer to external sources of support (such as a social worker, health professional or the police) in response to hypothetical dilemmas involving residents (r=0.48). Again, staff characteristics were the most important explanatory factors, accounting for just over a quarter of the variation in reported rates of criminal activity.

These analyses show associations, not causality, and there may be several explanations for observed relationships between rates of offending and staff to child ratios and vignette responses. Young people who engage in criminal behaviour are arguably more challenging to care for than those who do not, and so institutions with high rates of criminal offending among residents may use higher staff to child ratios to accommodate this challenging behaviour. Similarly, staff working in institutions with higher rates of criminal offending may be more likely to perceive a need to call on additional or specialized resources when faced with problematic situations. At the same time, however, the association between staff to child ratios and rates of offending could be interpreted in terms of the emphasis in pedagogic and attachment theory on relationship formation: an environment where a small number of young people live with a large number of staff may not be conducive to the formation of personalized relationships, and this in turn could create risk of disadvantage. Furthermore, in institutions where a large number of staff look after residents there may be a fragmentation of knowledge or responsibility for individual young people; research on parenting has shown that lack of knowledge about young people's everyday lives is associated with more high risk behaviour (e.g., Crouter et al. 2005). In this regard, the findings highlight issues discussed in Chapter 4 about the relative lack of voice and professional confidence of English residential care workers, when compared with their pedagogic counterparts in Denmark and to a lesser extent in Germany.

Community engagement

The heads of establishment were asked about several aspects of young people's involvement in the local community. Managers reported that Danish young people engaged less with local life than those in other countries – however, as we shall see in the next chapter, this account does not tally with young people's reports of visits from friends.

Most English and German managers reported that they considered it usual for young people to have friends locally (18/23 in England and 11/12 in Germany), in contrast to Denmark, where only 3 out of 12 said it was usual for young people to have local friends (p<0.001). A similar pattern was found for managers' reports of young people's involvement in community events and activities, although this did not reach statistical significance. A third of Danish managers (4/12) reported young people's participation in community activities, compared with about half of English (12/25), and two-thirds of German respondents (8/11). By contrast, all German and Danish managers reported that their institutions had regular contacts with other local residential units, compared with about two-thirds (14/22) of English managers (p<0.007). This may reflect the differing structure of residential provision in England, where there are fewer multisite residential providers than in Denmark or Germany.

Danish respondents were less likely to report difficulties with young people's involvement in community events (3/10 compared with 19/25 in England and 8/12 in Germany; p<0.05). This finding is perhaps not surprising – if Danish establishments are less involved with their local communities, they may be less likely to encounter problems. There were no cross-country differences in the reasons given by managers for difficulties with young people's involvement in the community. In England, the most commonly cited reason, mentioned by eight managers, for difficulty involving young people in community events was young people's reluctance to participate. Managers in all countries cited young people's characteristics as a further source of difficulty, often citing lack of confidence and low self-esteem, and two German managers referred to residents 'odd social behaviour' or 'strange' behaviour. Another German respondent commented that 'the social abilities of the young people are not developed enough; they don't believe they are capable to do this'. Two English respondents also commented on the risks posed to young people by their involvement in the local community; one said, 'this is a bad neighbourhood, which causes problems for young people and for [the establishment], [local people] lead them into trouble'.

In England, all heads of establishment were in regular contact with the police, compared with three-quarters (9/12) in Germany and less than half in Denmark (5/12; p<0.001). Perhaps that finding is unsurprising, given the higher rates of criminal offending among young people in England than in Denmark or Germany. Yet, it may also speak of the greater degree of marginalization experienced by English children in care with respect to mainstream society.

Discussion

The findings presented here show striking cross-country differences in outcome indicators for young people looked after. According to the reports of managers and young people themselves, those in residential care in England are, when compared to their Danish and German counterparts, more likely to be out of education and/or employment and at greater risk of teenage pregnancy and/or engagement in criminal activity. But what does this mean? Do the relatively better circumstances of Danish and German respondents reflect the benefits of pedagogic care work or are they instead a reflection of the young people's care entry characteristics or of wider population or societal differences between the countries? These intertwined sources of variation cannot be completely untangled by our research, but some insights may be obtained.

English residential provision differed structurally from that of the other countries. Settings accommodated fewer young people but had higher staff to child ratios (almost 4:1 in England, compared with a little over 2:1 in Germany and Denmark) and fewer children under 12 years of age. There were also differences in placement, with higher resident turnover in England, and a smaller proportion of locally placed young people. While almost half of Danish young people returned home at weekends, this was more unusual in Germany (only 25 percent went home for weekends) and England (15 percent). Reflecting the policy differences discussed earlier, English young people were more likely than their continental peers to have court ordered placements or placements where criminal behaviour was a precipitating factor. Together, this evidence reinforces an argument that we, as authors, have heard many times when discussing our research: in considering why English looked-after young people in residential care do worse than those in other European countries, we must recognize that we are not comparing like with like. Perhaps poorer outcome indicators for English young people reflect the fact that they are a more behaviourally challenging group, with greater disruption in terms of their placement history and their family circumstances.

In fact, regression analyses showed only limited evidence of links between variables that could be construed as 'characteristics of the care population' and as outcome indicators for young people. To take one example, in English establishments where a higher proportion of residents had visits from family members, young people aged 15 and over reported taking higher numbers of public examinations than in Denmark and Germany. It seems plausible that the proportion of residents receiving visits from family reflects residents' care histories, such that a higher degree of contact is associated with less troubled or traumatic family backgrounds. Residents with less troubled backgrounds might be expected to experience relatively less disadvantage in educational terms than those with more disrupted family relationships. However, when looking at results for all three countries together, contact with family was not a significant explanatory variable. The number of examinations taken by 15–18-year-olds was correlated with country, but also with managers' policies about higher education and staff perception of higher numbers of responsibilities towards young people in their care. In considering the results presented in this chapter as a whole, staff variables, which we would argue reflect the pedagogic approach, clearly played a more important role than those describing the establishment populations in explaining variance in outcome indicators for young people.

Staff differences across country were so pronounced in this study (see Chapters 4 and 5) that it became very difficult in analysis to untangle statistically the relative influence on outcome indicators of country and of the staff variables in question. For example, we initially sought to associate level of education among residential staff with outcome indicators for young people. However, this analysis was attempted with a dataset where almost all Danish workers had degree level qualifications in pedagogy, the majority of German workers had mid-level qualification, and almost no English workers had relevant degrees, with a minority holding low-level NVQ qualifications. Level of qualification acted as an almost perfect proxy for country, making it impossible to determine whether, for example, the relatively better outcomes seen among Danish young people were associated with their staff's pedagogy degrees, or with other characteristics of Denmark as a country.

Consideration of the relative influence of country and pedagogy needs also to take account of wider intercountry differences in population welfare and characteristics. As we noted at the beginning of this volume, our analysis – and our judgement of the value of social pedagogy – cannot ignore wider issues such as poverty, class and the welfare regimes of the countries included in the research, all of which provide a context for young people's lives and opportunities, as well as for residential care provision.

The Organisation for Economic Co-operation and Development (OECD 2005) publish annual statistics on a range of social indicators for its 30 member countries, which include the three that formed the subject of our investigation.[4] These general population data, summarized in Table 6.4, show similar patterns of cross-country difference to those observed among young people looked after in the present sample, with an overall trend suggesting that Denmark reports fewer difficulties than Germany, which in turn shows less population-level disadvantage than England.

The countries also differ in their relative spending on welfare services, as might be expected given their differing welfare models. In Denmark, spending on social services other than health comprises 5.4 percent of the GDP (Gross Domestic Product), compared with 2.6 percent in Germany and 1.2 percent in the UK (figures from 2001). The differences observed in our sample, for example in the proportions out of education and employment, or experiencing teenage pregnancy, in part reflect this wider social context, which probably accounts for some of our findings. For example, it might plausibly explain why 'care population' characteristics, such as the proportion of young people placed outside their local authority, do not account for significant variance in outcome indicators once country is taken into account – the stronger influence of country differences over-rides (and thus obscures) the weaker association.

Table 6.4: Whole population social indicators (whole population) (Simmons et al. (2002); OECD 2005)[1]

	England	Germany	Denmark
Child poverty (%):*	16.2	12.8	2.4
Fertility rates, 15–19-year-olds (%):	28.2	13.2	6.6
Average years of schooling, 25–64-year-olds:	13.3	13.4	12.7
15–19-year-olds not in education or employment (%):	8.6	4.7	2.4
Crimes committed per head of total population (2001 data):	0.106	0.077	0.088

Notes: *Share of children 17 years and under living in households with equivalized disposable income less than 50% of median income. [1]Raw data tables available at www.oecd.org/document/24/ 0,2340,en_2825_497118_2671576_1_1_1_1,00.html#raw (accessed 29 September 2005).

Given these observations, can we conclude from our data that a pedagogic approach to residential care work confers benefits for looked-after children and young people? After all, our cross-sectional research design precludes direct causal analysis. In Chapters 4 and 5, we described many differences between English, German and Danish workers, both in terms of workforce characteristics such as levels of in-service training, and in relation to their care work practice – for example their perceived responsibilities for young people in their care and strategies for dealing with hypothetical situations involving residents. The analyses reported in this chapter show that such differences are also related to variation in child outcome indicators, and indeed that staff characteristics provide a better explanation of variance in outcome indicators than country.

The observation that staff responses to hypothetical vignettes related to outcome indicators such as rates of pregnancy among young people under the age of 19 may be particularly relevant to our discussion of the value of pedagogy because it suggests that aspects of staff practice relate directly to young people's disadvantage or well-being. Two areas of staff response to vignettes accounted for significant variance in regression analyses – factually based responding, and reference to external sources of support.[5] Overall, analyses presented in Chapter 5 showed that English workers were least likely to suggest 'fact seeking' responses to hypothetical dilemmas, that is to seek additional information from the child about the situation in question. At the same time, they were more likely than German or Danish workers to suggest seeking external help and advice or to refer the child to an external agency. In our discussion of these data earlier in the book, we have suggested that the pedagogic approach may be more focused on the young person as an individual, rather than on a collection of problems or behaviours that need to be managed. This notion ties back to Meins and colleagues' (2002) conception of mind-mindedness, as a form of sensitive responsiveness, and a key part of the attachment relationship. Undoubtedly, we must recognize that these relationships are not causal, and that staff strategies will partly reflect cross-country differences in care populations and in regulated procedures around staff practice. That said, it is noteworthy – but perhaps not surprising – that less 'child-centred' or pedagogic care strategies were associated with higher rates of disadvantage in the present sample of young people – arguably those who would benefit from it most.

We have already observed that many aspects of current English policy for children and young people, including those in care, are pedagogic in their rhetoric. For example, just as the young person's developing independence and fulfilment of his or her potential are central to pedagogic work in continental European residential care, these principles are emphasized in policy documents such as the National Minimum Standards for Children's Homes (2000) in England and Wales, the *Children Act* (2004). Similar principles are detailed in Scottish legislation, including the *National Care Standards for Care Homes for Children and Young People* (2000), in relation to the *Children (Scotland) Act* (1995). A key outcome target within the *English Care Standards Act* (2000) is that 'Children receive care which helps prepare them for and support them into adulthood'. Standards specifically require provision of individually appropriate personal, health, social and sex education for young residents and services aimed at developing individual identity. The question for England – indeed for the UK – is how such principled objectives can be met. Arguably the breadth of pedagogic training is uniquely placed to ensure that residential care providers are qualified to meet these objectives.

UK policy also emphasizes young people's consultation and collaboration in plans for their care. For example, the Department of Health has sponsored Children's Rights Officers and Advocates (CROA) to develop training materials for local authorities and other agencies, so they can devise practical strategies for young people's participation in service provision (CROA 2000). One focus of this material is decision-making around care plans, including where to live and who to live with. The *National Minimum Standards for Children's Homes* (2000) set out systems for consultation about key decisions affecting children's lives, and regulations specify that children's opinions about everyday matters should also be considered. These regulations have parallels with pedagogic policies in other countries, but we are some way from the levels of collaborative work reported in other countries visited (e.g., Denmark, the Netherlands), where formal structures such as youth councils exist to involve young people in policy making, and there are legal requirements for consultation and consent in care planning.

The analyses presented here have shown the significance of staff characteristics in relation to outcome indicators for looked-after young people, but to make this observation is not to 'blame' residential care workers for the relative disadvantage of English young people when compared with their Danish and German peers. Rather, the wider context in which English residential care workers are trained and conduct their practice must be recognized. The differences we have described are not simply about workers' professionality, or pedagogic education, but are rooted in the policies, welfare regimes and cultural context of the countries studied.

Pedagogy, as it is understood in continental Europe, provides a coherent and well-established discourse underpinning policy and practice for all children, including those looked after. As the above examples indicate, policies for children and young people in care in Denmark and Germany are explicitly pedagogic, as is the legal requirement for a professionally educated workforce. Although the professionalization of the residential care workforce and the development of education is less advanced in England than in Denmark or Germany, the education of the workforce and the creation of a more coherent framework of qualifications for work with children are English government priorities. English policy documents such as *Every Child Matters* (DfES 2003) and the Children Act (2004)[6] contain ideas and recommendations that accord with social pedagogic principles, such as 'educating through and for society and communities' (Hämäläinen 2003: 73). Indeed, at the time of writing, one model being considered for the children's workforce in England was that of the pedagogue (DfES 2005). The analyses described in this chapter suggest that the professionalization of the workforce, through pedagogic education, would be associated with better life chances for looked-after young people, in terms of outcome indicators such as participation in education and employment, rates of teenage pregnancy and of criminal behaviour.

While the findings presented in this chapter are striking, a focus on the 'traditional' outcome indicators discussed here would mean that we, as authors, were failing to adopt a pedagogic approach to understanding the lives of young people participating in the research. In the next chapter we will attempt, as researchers, to adopt a *Lebensweltorientierung* – a living world orientation – that is, to consider evidence for the benefits of a pedagogic approach in terms of young people's views of their everyday lives, their relationships with staff and something of their experience of the social worlds in which they live.

Notes

1 Data were missing from some heads of establishment, due to incomplete questionnaire responses in some instances, and to establishment characteristics – for example some units did not have any residents aged 16 and over.

In addition, seven German unit managers completed questionnaires but were not interviewed – the head of the whole establishment was interviewed instead – and these seven cases have been treated as missing for all analyses involving head interview data. As a consequence, numbers – and hence statistical power – were limited for some analyses, and are reported for each analysis separately.

2   Correlational analyses look at the strength of the relationship between two variables (e.g., height and shoe size) to produce a correlation (r), which varies between 0 and 1. The stronger the relationship between the two variables, the closer the correlation is to 1. Multiple linear regression can be used to learn more about the relationship between several independent or predictor variables and one dependent or outcome variable. Linear regression produces a statistic called 'adjusted R^2', which refers to the proportion of variation in the outcome variable that is explained (statistically) by the predictor variables, and which again varies between 0 and 1, depending on the strength of the relationship. For example, if adjusted R^2 is equal to 0.4, then 40 percent of the variation in an outcome variable (called the 'variance') can be explained by its relationship with the predictor variables. Perhaps most important to remember is that these analyses describe *relationships* between different variables – they do not show cause and effect.

3   The GCSE is a General Certificate in Secondary Education, based on approximately two years of study, and assessed from grades A* to G on the basis of coursework and public examination.

4   OECD (2005) data refer to the United Kingdom, and not to England separately.

5   Other facets of vignette responses were also associated with outcome indicators for young people, but these variables were, not surprisingly, highly intercorrelated, and so the effect of those less strongly related to outcome indicators effectively 'washed out' of regression equations.

6   Available at http://www.opsi.gov.uk/acts/acts2004/20040031.htm (accessed 11 May 2006).

7 Looked-after lives

Introduction

It is now time to turn to the children and young people themselves and to take a closer look at what they had to say about their experience of residential care. We come to them last not because they are least important but because we thought that their accounts require the detailed context provided by the earlier chapters.

Earlier chapters in this section have described the policy, practice and organizational background for residential care in Denmark, Germany and England. We have seen the important ways in which residential establishments differed between the different countries: how, in the English settings, there was rather less stability of staff, and how staff in Denmark were most qualified, in England least qualified, with staff in Germany having an intermediate position. We have also seen that in many ways, pedagogues in Germany and Denmark took a rather more personal or relational, rather than procedural, approach to the work and to the children in their care. In particular, we have seen that the young people in the English establishments studied were less advantaged in many ways than their counterparts in Denmark and Germany. In terms of policy, we also know that, overall, there are good reasons for thinking that children in English residential care represent a more disadvantaged group than in the other two countries.

All of the above dissimilarities suggest between country differences in children's histories as well as in their current social contexts. They are likely to affect some of the findings arising from the interviews with children and young people, which we describe in this chapter.

In the course of our work, we did not ask young people about their care history: this was not the aim of the study, although their previous experience may well have influenced how they evaluated their current situation. We asked, instead, about their everyday lives as residents of a children's home, about the sort of activities which they enjoyed and about what they thought of staff. We enquired as to their participation in decisions about daily activities and the extent to which they mixed with young people who were not fellow residents. The interviews revealed something of young people's appraisal of their experience of living in a children's home, their reports of whom they turned to in difficulties, their interactions with staff and other residents and their daily activities. We will find that in some ways young people's views are rather similar in the three countries that we studied but that there are some notable differences.

Issues of stability

We begin by considering young people's relationships and interactions with staff. Part of the context for relationships with staff concerns the duration of young people's placements and, alongside this, stability among the staff group.

Having stable, long-term relationships with staff is important because it is only over time that young people can gain enough information about another person (to 'learn' about them, as it were), so as to know whether or not they are worthy of trust. This applies to other residents and, as we shall consider first, members of staff. In England, as we have seen, there was a higher ratio of staff to young people than in Denmark and Germany. It could be that this provides a better opportunity for developing closer relationships between staff and young people, although a different way of looking at it is, maybe, to say that residents have more staff to come to terms with. In addition, the greater instability of placement, and the greater turnover among staff may undermine any advantage to be obtained from higher staff ratios. One young woman in England said:

> I would say [*to a new resident*] don't tell [staff your] personal business, don't trust them, that they know too much about you. As soon as you leave they're not your friends, you're not allowed back. Other [young people] told me not to trust staff when I came [here].

With an experience of instability, of relationships that come and go, it must be difficult to commit oneself to trust the people with whom one lives. A long-term relationship, on the other hand, allows those concerned enough knowledge to be able to predict, to some extent, the other's likely response in a variety of circumstances, as the following examples bear out.

A young man, aged 17, in a German residential home, said of staff:

> They are good. One has to come to know them, learn their language, learn to understand things ... You get quite a good life [here], you come to understand your life.

A 15-year-old, in Denmark, when asked what she would tell a new resident about staff, casts some light on how staff changes can be unsettling:

I think I would describe [them] as nice. Before [the staff changes] . . .
they were nice and helpful, now it is a strange relationship. The old
ones – if they were here, then I would be so happy. They were genius,
now the new ones are here they have a strange way of working.

And a member of staff in a Danish establishment, answering a question
about whether staff had responsibility to advise young people said:

I think they are very open, and often they come themselves and ask
for help; especially the ones who have been here for a longer time
and who feel secure and have confidence in us.

Staff: a source of support?

In the course of everyday life, and in situations where young people need
someone to turn to, staff would seem to be in the frontline. While, clearly,
staff are not the young people's parents, they are the primary caregivers for
the young people during their time in the establishment, with responsibilities
for many of the everyday tasks involved in parenting. Here, we look first at
whether young people would go to staff when problems arose, if they would
advise other young people to do so and, connected to this, their general
appraisal of staff. We will turn to other sources of support, later.

It is important that young people have someone to turn to when they are
experiencing difficulties. In answer to the question: 'If you had something on
your mind or had a problem, whom would you choose to talk to about it . . . Is
there anyone else you would talk to?' (Table 7.1), it is encouraging that 82
percent of young people in all three countries indicated that they would
speak to a member of staff about any problems, with no statistically significant differences between countries. Seventy percent (201) of young people
thought they could talk to staff and that they were good at listening, 74
percent (222) said that staff treated them with respect and 67 percent (201)
thought that staff listened to their point of view. Analysis of variance looking
at mean scores for these questions (see below) did not reveal statistically
significant differences between countries.

However, a rather less positive picture emerged from responses to a later
question about whether young people would advise new residents to speak to
staff if they had any problems. Twenty-three percent of the young people in
England would *not* advise taking problems to staff, compared to 13 percent
(15) of those in Germany and 10 percent (8) in Denmark. The responses to
this question were scored 1 where the interviewee answered 'no', 2 if there
was an ambivalent response and 3 if they replied with a straight 'yes': the
mean rank of scores in England was 134, in Germany, 154 and in Denmark,
152 (this pattern just failed to reach statistical significance; $p < 0.07$).[1]

Table 7.1: Young people's responses to, 'If you had something on your mind or had a problem, whom would you choose to talk to about it ... Is there anyone else you would talk to?' by country

Person young person would speak to	England N (%)	Germany N (%)	Denmark N (%)	Total (%)
Member of staff:†	74 (83)	89 (77)	71 (87)	234 (82)
Non-resident professional:†	17 (19)	10 (9)	8 (10)	35 (12)
Resident friend:†	21 (24)	25 (22)	28 (34)	74 (26)
Non-resident friend:**	21 (24)	55 (49)	31 (38)	107 (38)
family member:*	27 (30)	47 (42)	46 (56)	120 (42)
Other:	3 (3)	6 (5)	4 (5)	13 (5)
Total:	89 (100)	113 (100)	82 (100)	284 (100)
Missing cases:	11 (–)	3 (–)	4 (–)	18 (–)

Notes: † Not significant; * p<0.01; ** p<0.001. A multiple response table: young people could have reported more than one thing they spoke to staff about. Therefore columns may not sum to 100%.

We then asked about anything young people would tell new residents about staff. There were some who answered, understandably, that they would prefer not to speak to new residents about staff, because newcomers should form their own opinions. Nevertheless, the accounts of those who would proffer advice give something of the flavour of the lives of young people in care and what they think about the people with whom they live. Analysis of their replies showed a range of positive, negative and mixed responses. The following list of examples allows the children and young people to speak for themselves, representing their views in their own words. Some answers included a completely positive view of staff:

> [They are] lovely, I love them all to bits, I think they're brilliant and trustworthy.
>
> (England)

> I would say you can talk to them like a social worker, but they're better than social workers ... nothing else.
>
> (England)

> That they understand everything, that they have already been through it, they are very sympathetic...
>
> (Germany)

> That they are kind.
>
> (Germany)

They are very helpful. They cannot always help, but then they refer to somebody else or ask you to wait 'til the following day. They are people who have surplus energy for you – which I have not always experienced at home.

(Denmark)

Rather more answers, however, revealed a mixed or a negative view of staff.

One is nice, some act like they just come to get the money and go home, act like they care but don't.

(England)

Most of them are bastards and some not.

(Germany)

They're generally all right but they take too long to do things, just sit out back having a fag when they could be helping us out and wonder why we get pissed off.

(England)

There are some [pedagogues] who are not good at this kind of job, do not know about children and young people.

(Denmark)

Of course there are some of the adults that I like better

(Denmark)

[I] would tell her who was good and who wasn't, some can keep secrets and some can't because they write it down in the book in the office, and I don't like it.

(England)

In a similar vein to the last speaker, a German resident spoke of the 'dishonesty of staff' saying that 'things that have nothing to do with anyone are talked through by the staff'. These are examples of children who believed that their trust had been betrayed by staff, other examples of this arose in response to other questions. Because of their complex responsibilities and roles, staff have a delicate path to tread. For residents, they are 'familiar', that is to some extent they share the young people's living space and they are often playful and open in their interactions with young people. They may, therefore, be perceived by residents as 'friends'. A few young people, in all three countries (seven in England, two in Germany and eight in Denmark) when asked what they enjoyed doing with staff, referred especially to having fun. 'We play fighting and mess around', 'Have a laugh', 'Romping around', 'Taking the piss', 'Fight in fun with one of the men pedagogues'. Rather similar proportions of young people in all three countries said that most of the staff were fun to be with (56 percent (50) of the young people in England, 57 percent (66) of the young people in Germany and 55 percent (44) of the young people in Denmark). These differences were not statistically significant.

Occasionally, in answer to the same question and elsewhere, the young people referred to their care workers or pedagogues as being like themselves. Two English young people replied: 'You treat them like they are one of the kids', and 'Staff are like kids ... they are sort of adults knowing what it's like to be a kid, not the sort [of adult] you'd be embarrassed be seen in street with, but responsible. They respect you, meet half way, they are not like old people'.

People who work in residential homes need to be responsible adults, but residents also appreciate it if they can interact less seriously, making less of hierarchical differences between themselves and the young people with whom they work. At the same time they have obligations to act as professionals, promoting the children's best interests in ways which the young people themselves may not immediately appreciate. For example, they invite residents' confidences while reserving the right to disclose these, as appropriate. This is an area of work for residential staff that, like much else, requires sensitivity, self-knowledge and the ability to combine professional distance and reflection with a personal, relational approach, without compromising either. These are issues addressed directly in pedagogic training.

A few young people spontaneously commented that life in the residential home was better than that in their own homes, or that staff treated them with greater respect than did their parents. A young woman in England, said, 'It's like having five or six parents, that they care for you ...' She clearly appreciated her relationship with staff. At the same time, her reply gives rise to a question: what is it be like to live with five, six or more parent figures, some of whom you like and some you don't, coming and going, during the course of the day and of the week?

Sometimes the negative view of staff expressed by some young people overlapped with advice and warnings about how the new resident should be wary of certain staff, and about how they should conduct themselves in order to avoid staff displeasure. Sometimes information about 'acceptable' behaviour and observing establishment rules did not seem to be proffered in any spirit of criticism of staff, merely as friendly advice from 'old hands' to newcomers, at other times it was more disapproving:

> Make sure you catch staff you want to speak to when they're in a good mood, otherwise they might take it out on you.
>
> (England)

You should be careful with certain things [like] loud music. Watch their facial expressions!

(Germany)

They are relaxed, but they don't like [you] skipping school, there are clear rules which one has to follow.

(Germany)

I think that they are nice sometimes. Sometimes they can be strict . . . when you do not listen to them – but it is . . . okay, because we have to listen to what they say.

(Denmark)

Their answers provide glimpses into these young people's lives and their relationship with staff. Staff may sometimes be perceived as capricious – they have moods, attracting their anger is to be avoided and a substantial group of young people do not fully trust them. Nevertheless, between one-half and two-thirds of young people across the three countries said that most of the staff were fair, and between 66 and 71 percent said that most of the staff were reliable. Between country differences in the above findings are not significantly different.

Enjoying leisure activities with staff

Most young people, but particularly those in Danish establishments, reported that they enjoyed activities undertaken with staff, whether individually or with a group of residents. Eighty-seven percent (72) of young people in Denmark enjoyed group activities led by staff, compared to 74 percent (72) for England and 71 percent (82) for Germany (p<0.03). Eighty-four percent (70) of young people in Denmark, compared to 63 percent (71) in Germany and 69 percent (69) in England said that they enjoyed doing things with a member of staff (p<0.005).

In answer to these questions, the young people living in Danish establishments were more positive than those living in English and German establishments. In fact, throughout the interview, the young people in Denmark mostly gave a more positive account of their experience than did the other two groups, a pattern that was consistent whether or not differences reached statistical significance.

Where applicable, we asked young people about the sort of activities which they enjoyed doing with staff. The following categories were derived from their answers and post-coded: physical activities and sport; indoor games; talking and enjoying the companionship of staff; outings; watching television, videos and DVDs; holidays; fun and playfulness; practical and creative skills together; homework and other educational tasks. Young people in Denmark mentioned more activities and more categories of activity than those in England or Germany in responding to this question. The young people in Denmark mentioned 2.88 (sd=1.90) categories of activity on average, compared to 1.54 (sd=1.48) for those in England and 1.10 (sd=1.23) for those interviewed in Germany (p=0.001).

Enjoying companionship and talking to staff was specifically mentioned by one-third of all the young people we interviewed: by 48 percent (42) of those living in Danish establishments, 33 percent (32) of those living in English establishments and 23 percent (27) of those living in German establishments (p<0.001). For example, in Germany a resident said that he liked to discuss his future with staff; another said they liked talking about problems and 'general matters' and another that they liked going to a café with the pedagogue and talking. A boy in an English residential home said, 'I smoke with staff, I just go out and have a talk when they have smoke' (smoking is not permitted indoors in the establishment); and another, 'I just like the company of the staff'; and a third said, 'I socialize with them too, talk about any worries'.

A resident in Denmark said, 'Sometimes they will help me to tidy my room. Now, they do not help so much, they will sit on my bed and tell me to start [tidying]. It is cosy'. And another, 'They give me a massage, we watch television and have a cosy time when the small children have been put to bed.' Another young person in Denmark said that what she enjoyed with staff was, 'playing hide and seek in the whole house, play games, watch television together [and] when the group is together and we have *afternoon-good-time* [a designated time when the group got together to enjoy each other's company, drink tea and eat cakes]. Eleven of the young people interviewed in Denmark referred, spontaneously, to 'cosiness' when talking about their preferred activities with staff, none of the young people in the other two countries did so. Cosiness is a term that speaks of domesticity, a feeling of physical and social ease, in contrast to the more institutional characteristics and control that emerged from other accounts.

While companionship was not always mentioned explicitly, when residents spoke of what they enjoyed doing with staff it may well have been one element in their enjoyment of other activities. It is noticeable that the young people in Denmark show greater appreciation than those in England and Germany, and that those in English establishments are, for the most part, somewhat higher in their appreciation than those in German establishments.

For example, when it came to indoor leisure time activities, indoor games with staff were enjoyed by 43 percent (38) of young people in Denmark, 31 percent (30) in England and 19 percent (22) in Germany (p=0.001). Watching television with staff was enjoyed by 24 percent (21) of in Denmark, 13 percent (13) in England and 4 percent (5) in Germany (p<0.001).

A few young people replied that they enjoyed doing homework or other formal educational activities with staff: 6 percent (7) in Germany, 4 percent (5) in Denmark, but none in England (p<0.001). Although these are small numbers, it is interesting that educational matters should be represented as favoured activities at all. The findings may relate to establishment policies about supporting children's schooling, discussed in the last chapter, and the greater likelihood for those in English establishments to be out of education.

Out of doors, taking part in sports and physical activities such as football, cycling and swimming with staff were mentioned appreciatively by 32 percent (28) of young people interviewed in Danish establishments, 24 percent (23) of those interviewed in English establishments and 15 percent (17) of those interviewed in Germany (p<0.02).

Creative and practical activities were also mentioned by some of the young people. Their accounts suggested that pedagogues in Denmark appeared to be more able to engage in practical activities with the young people than their colleagues in Germany or England, and to do so in such a way that the young people remembered the activities with enjoyment. Twenty-five percent (22) of young people interviewed in Denmark compared to 7 percent (8) in Germany and 5 percent (5) in England spoke about enjoying skills and creative activities with the staff (p<0.001). This finding supports the argument that the practical and creative component of the pedagogy degree equips residential care workers to engage with young people through joint activities. The five English young people who said they enjoyed practical activities with staff all mentioned taking part in cooking. In the other countries, as well as cooking, residents referred to learning woodwork, carrying out repairs in the house such as putting up shelves, decorating rooms, gardening and paving a path.

In answer to the same open question about the sort of activities which they enjoyed doing with staff, outings with staff were also mentioned appreciatively by 35 percent of young people in Denmark, 12 percent (12) in England and 12 percent (14) in Germany (p=0.001). Such outings ranged from fairly low key expeditions, such as shopping, to excursions further afield: '[We] go to the park, I like doing things with N., she's fun' (young person in England); 'Going to the cinema, to exhibitions, to a café' (young person in Germany); 'Sometimes, when all the pedagogues are here, we go for a bus ride on the road along the coast, to buy ice cream' (young person in Denmark).

Going on holiday together with other people in the establishment was also remembered as an enjoyable activity, in answer to the same open question and was mentioned by 8 percent of those interviewed in Denmark and 3 percent of those interviewed in Germany. Appreciation of joint holidays was mentioned in response to other questions. This was not the case for any of the English children, unsurprisingly given that few of them had been away on holiday with the group.

Table 7.2: Holidays taken by young people in the last year

Young people on holiday with	England N (%)	Germany N (%)	Denmark N (%)	Total N (%)
Establishment:***	40 (42)	62 (54)	77 (92)	179 (61)
Parents:*	7 (7)	16 (14)	19 (23)	42 (14)
School:**	4 (4)	7 (6)	14 (17)	25 (9)
Non-resident friends:†	2 (2)	8 (7)	8 (10)	18 (6)
Other relatives:†	4 (4)	7 (6)	10 (12)	21 (7)
Other:**	9 (9)	33 (29)	17 (20)	59 (20)
Not known:	0 (0)	3 (3)	1 (1)	4 (1)
Not been on holiday:***	34 (35)	16 (14)	0 (0)	50 (17)
Total number of cases:	96 (100)	114 (100)	84 (100)	294 (100)
Missing cases:	4	2	2	8

Notes: † p<0.10 non significant trend; * p<0.05; ** p<0.01; *** p<0.001. A multiple response table: young people could have reported going on holiday with more than one person/organization. Therefore columns may not sum to 100%.

In fact, the English children were much less likely to have been on holiday at all in the past year, as their answers to a different question revealed.

Table 7.2 shows that many young people had been on a group holiday with staff and fellow residents: 92 percent (77) of those living in Danish establishments, 54 percent (62) of those in German establishments and 42 percent (40) of those in English establishments. Moreover, when prompted as to whether they had been on holiday with anyone else in the last 12 months, for every category of person or groups with whom they might have holidayed (friends, family, school and others) the Danish children and young people scored higher than the other two groups, while the English children responded less positively over all the categories. A third of the English young people (35 percent) said they had not been on holiday at all over the past year. Also only 7 percent (7) had been away with their parents, compared with twice as many German and more than three times as many Danish young people.

The high proportion of children in Denmark indicating that they had been on holiday with other people from their establishment speaks of the value that Danish policy and the pedagogic approach place on young people's collective life – although, as Table 7.2 shows, many of the children in Danish residential homes had other holiday opportunities as well. In this aspect of their lives, as in others, the young people living in Denmark appeared less disadvantaged than the others and especially than those in English residential care.

Staff making a difference to young people's lives?

Young people were asked whether they considered the staff had made a difference to their lives in any way. Again we rated their answers in terms of whether they replied in positive, mixed or negative terms. The majority said staff had made a positive difference to their lives although this was reported by fewer of those interviewed in England (57 percent; n=51) than in Germany (66 percent; n=74) or in Denmark (71 percent; n=55). The remainder said either that staff had made no difference or they answered in mixed terms. A very few young people, overall, said that staff had changed their lives for the worse (4 percent).

Next, we asked the young people to specify the sorts of changes that staff had made. The young people gave a wide range of responses. Many of them referred to an improvement in attitude or behaviour, including at school. For example:

Young people in England

> [They] probably taught me to trust more than when I was in foster care. When I was taken from my mum, I didn't trust anyone, I thought I was being unloyal to my mum. I was 11 years old then; I trust the staff here, now.

> Some have tried to encourage me, told me if I keep doing my school work everything will be alright. I think about it but I don't know if it helps...

> Made me better behaved, increased my maturity. They [give] you your own space and stuff, but set rules, help make us behave, and we get rewards. [The] system is fair.

Young people in Germany

> [I] became more sensible, kind with people, pay more attention to myself. [I] get along better with my parents. My room is always tidied up. School has got better, too.

> I'm better at school, my appearance, how I have to look on the street, how to behave. They've let me develop well and thrive in these five years. They have shown me how I can cope later.

I wasn't in school for two years, before. Alone, I wouldn't have found the strength to go [to school] again.

My behaviour changed, I am less aggressive and in a bad mood. In the past, I frequently wasn't at school. I became more independent. I became more open regarding talking about problems or in general, too.

Young people in Denmark

[They've made] a big difference, before I could only see the bad things, there were only bad things, the fear to come back from school and be beaten up [at home]. For that reason I am happy to be here. I have learnt to see things in a positive way, to see the bright side.

First of all I have become more open, I dare talk about problems; I could not do that before. [I'm] more mature, I learnt about being more independent and to make different decisions. They made me to know about the real world from another side [perspective] than [that of] my parents.

I have got a better relationship with my mother and father since I came here.

Thirteen of the children interviewed in Denmark and Germany, overall, spoke of being supported in their relationship with their families, while none of the English children did so. In earlier chapters, we described how pedagogues in Germany and Denmark were more likely to have a responsibility for working with parents, than those working in English establishments. Also staff reported more contact between children and their families in Germany and Denmark than in England.

Making decisions

The importance of involving young people in decision-making relates to the significance for young people's well-being of caregiving that is relational and 'mind-minded', as we discussed in Chapter 1, recognizing the 'other' as a person in their own right. We did not ask what young people thought about the way in which the major decisions about their lives had been made. These depend to a greater extent on outside agencies rather than on the head and staff of residential institutions. We did, however, ask about how more everyday decisions were made.

We asked young people about a variety of possibilities regarding their involvement in decision-making (Table 7.3). We prompted them as to whether there were possibilities for this in more formal settings, mentioning children's councils and regular meetings of what we called the 'living group' – that is the immediate group of children and staff with whom they shared their lives. We also asked about informal group and individual conversations and whether these were occasions for making decisions about everyday activities.

Table 7.3: Ways in which the young people report making decisions about their day-to-day lives within the establishment

Ways in which the young people can make decisions about their day-to-day lives within the establishment	England N (%)	Germany N (%)	Denmark N (%)	Total N (%)
None:*	13 (13)	9 (8)	2 (2)	24 (8)
Children's council (all young people):**	9 (9)	7 (6)	20 (24)	36 (12)
Regular meetings of living group:**	38 (39)	42 (38)	57 (68)	137 (47)
Other regular meeting of whole group:**	41 (42)	26 (23)	7 (8)	74 (25)
Informal discussion with living group staff:**	22 (23)	52 (46)	53 (63)	127 (43)
Informal discussion with other staff:**	5 (5)	29 (26)	23 (27)	57 (19)
Other (e.g. that they decide for themselves):**	2 (2)	21 (19)	17 (20)	40 (14)
Don't know:†	1 (1)	2 (2)	2 (2)	5 (2)
Total number of cases:	97 (100)	112 (100)	84 (100)	293 (100)
Missing cases:	3	4	2	9

Notes: † Not significant; * $p<0.05$; ** $p<0.001$.

Thirteen percent (13) of the residents in English establishments, 8 percent (9) in German and 2 percent (2) in Danish establishments replied that there were no ways in which they made decisions about their lives. For those young people who reported having at least one way of making decisions, a score was created representing the number of different ways for making decisions about their everyday lives (ranging from one to six). Young people in Denmark reported more ways of making decisions (mean=2.13; sd=1.00) than those in Germany (mean=1.62; sd=1.05) or England (mean=1.2; sd=0.83; $p<0.001$).

Young people were asked how satisfied they were with the ways in which decisions were made in the establishment, with responses scored '1' (not satisfied), '2' (ambivalent) or '3' (satisfied). Comparison of ranked scores[2] indicated that young people in England were significantly less satisfied with the ways in which everyday decisions were made than those interviewed in Germany and Denmark (p<0.02).

Young people's overall appraisal of staff

The interview ended with a series of questions designed to obtain the young people's overall appraisal of staff; these questions were intended, both individually (reported earlier in this chapter) and when summed together, to provide some indication of how young people appraised the establishment they lived in and the staff who worked there. We asked whether young people would talk to a member of staff if they had something on their mind and, if so, how helpful they had found this. We went on to enquire how good staff were at talking things through or at listening when the young person had something on their mind. We wanted to know if they would advise a new resident to talk to staff if they had a problem, believing that this would provide some indication of how they themselves regarded staff. Another question addressed whether young people thought that staff had made a difference to their lives, in any way and another if staff treated them with respect, including a question about how good staff were at listening to the young people's points of view. We asked whether they thought that staff were mostly fair, whether some staff were fair or whether no staff were fair, and used a similar format to find out whether they thought that staff were reliable. Young people were also asked whether most, some or no staff were fun to be with.

The above items were grouped for analysis, with three average scores obtained for each country for positive, negative and mixed responses.[3] Only the variable summing negative responses differed significantly across countries, with Denmark's young people giving a lower summed negative appraisal of staff (mean=0.7; sd=1.4) than those in Germany (mean=1.0; sd=1.5) or England (mean=0.9; sd=1.5; p<0.05). This result is consistent with earlier findings in suggesting that young people in Denmark are less negative in their views of their residential care staff than those in other countries.

A similar pattern was found in the summed positive and mixed/ ambivalent appraisals of staff, although these comparisons just failed to reach statistical significance. Young people in Denmark gave somewhat higher positive ratings of staff (mean= 6.9; sd=3.2) than those in England (mean=6.5; sd=3.4) or Germany (mean=6.7; sd=2.7; p<0.10). For the mixed/ambivalent summed rating, the average for England was 2.7 (sd=2.4), for Germany 2.7 (sd=1.9) and for Denmark 2.9 (sd=2.5) (p<0.10).

Overall, however, differences across the three countries in young people's appraisals of staff were not pronounced, and this may speak of the extent to which looked-after children are willing to express themselves openly, whether to praise or to be critical, about those on whom they may be most dependent. As researchers we had assured interviewees that their replies would be treated as confidential, with the important proviso that if anything they said led us to believe that they were at risk, we would discuss it with them and perhaps take it further (see methodology). We cannot know, precisely, how they saw our role – even though we had prepared 'child-friendly' information sheets about the project. However, an educated guess would say that they placed us somewhere in, or relating to, the official world of social work and residential care. There were several instances, in answer to open questions about their relationships with staff, where young people remarked that staff cannot entirely be trusted with confidential information, and that they pass it on to other members of the staff group or to social workers, as we noted earlier.

Support from people who are not staff

The extent to which children feel they can turn to other people for support is important for their well-being, both now and for the future. They may turn to a range of people as well as to staff. As we have seen, attachment relationships are not confined to biological parents, nor to those who have day-to-day care of young people. Young people may have friends, both fellow residents and others in the outside community; some, although less so in England than in the other two countries, maintain contact with their families; they also know, and may trust, social workers, teachers and other professionals. We asked residents, 'If you had something on your mind or had a problem, to whom would you choose to talk about it? . . . Is there anyone else you would talk to?' We prompted for each of the categories shown in Table 7.1. The 'Other' shown in the table category includes a few who referred to their girlfriend or boyfriend, or gave answers as varied as 'God' and 'a website chat room'.

The table shows that for almost every category young people in England were less likely to respond that they had someone in whom they could confide. The exception, which does not reach statistical significance, was that some of them replied that they would confide in a professional worker not employed in the establishment. Otherwise, they were much less likely than the young people in Denmark or Germany to have people to turn to outside the establishment, whether friends or members of their family. They were also less likely to turn to the staff or young people with whom they lived.

Support from family members

Young people in Germany and Denmark were more likely to report that they would confide in a family member (41 percent, n=47, and 54 percent, n=46, respectively) than those in England (27 percent, n=27) (p<0.001). There may be many reasons behind this difference. First, there are the differences between the populations studied and it may be that the more extreme circumstances of young people interviewed in England make them less willing to confide in family members, or may mean that their contact with them has broken down; we saw in Chapter 6 that young people in England were more likely to have court order placements, and less likely to have contact with family than their counterparts in Denmark and Germany. At the same time, as noted in Chapter 5, a higher proportion of pedagogues in Denmark saw themselves as responsible for liaison with families, compared with those in England and Germany. The role of the family and rights of parents differ in different countries, nevertheless as Hill (2000: 60), in reviewing theories and models of residential care, notes:

> The rationale for promoting more family-centred approaches must take account of parents' rights and responsibilities, and of the pressures and problems they faced. However it must ultimately be based on children's needs and rights – to family belonging, continuity identity, choice

Hill concludes that, while in some circumstances it is not in a child's interests to promote family contact, in the great majority of cases legislation, theory and research favour maximizing family inclusion (Hill 2000).

In England, 64 percent of heads of residential homes said that families did not visit regularly, compared with 44 percent of heads in Germany and 17 percent in Denmark. They also reported a lower level of contact, such as phone calls, between families and children. There seems to have been little improvement in this respect since the study by Sinclair and Gibbs (1998), which reported that the great majority of children in residential care wanted to be in frequent touch with their families (though not to live with them), but that this was only achieved for a minority.

Support from fellow residents and friends

Table 7.1 also reveals differences in the extent to which young people identified members of their peer group as sources of support when they were worried about something. Three-quarters of the young people interviewed said they would not confide in a fellow resident. We did not ask why this was the case. However, answers to other questions provided some clues. For example in England, a girl who was asked what she would tell a newly arrived child about staff, replied instead in terms of her feelings about her peers, expressing extreme mistrust of the other residents:

> I would say all the kids are gone in head. I don't like them, I don't talk to kids in care, I don't trust them, I keep the door locked. Kids wouldn't come near me they wouldn't dare, they know I don't like them.

Others in England occasionally spoke of violent situations. For example:

> [There are] big arguments between kids and staff and between kids. I was bit for trying to stop the argument so I ended up in the fight. The girl who started it blamed it on me. Staff grabbed my arms and put them behind my back and said 'Breathe, breathe'.

The mix of young people who find themselves in residential establishments in England can create persistent problems, as Sinclair and Gibbs (1998) report. They found that most of the unhappy experiences that children reported arose from hostile relationships with other residents and being drawn by other residents (as they saw it) into self-harming or anti-social behaviour. In our study, one young woman alluded to her own violent behaviour and to what she saw as a threat of violence from the member of staff:

> One of the staff threatened me. I said I would punch her and she said 'You don't know people I know', but generally they respect me, they take me for who I am, a young woman, [*although I*] act a disturbed kid. They try not to judge, you are continually judged in care...

In Germany a young person, again in answer to a question about whether staff respected young people, said that they did not and gave the following as an example:

> A friend had to take his medicine and they forced him to do so. They held him and opened his mouth. That is because he throws a wobbly, or takes knives, if he doesn't take his medicine.

Disturbing events, such as these involving other residents, are not likely to inspire trust and friendship among young people. However, these examples are only part of the picture. When we asked people, directly, if they enjoyed spare time activities with other young people in their establishment: 80 percent (79) of young people in England, 82 percent (94) of young people in Germany and 93 percent (77) of young people in Denmark said that they did. In fact, they were rather more positive about doing things with other young people, than they were about activities with staff. Also, as we have already noted, many young people reported that they enjoyed group activities with fellow residents that were facilitated by staff. Again, young people in Denmark gave more positive accounts: 87 percent (72) said they enjoyed group activities compared with 72 percent (72) for England and 71 percent (82) for Germany (p<0.05).

Children in residential care may also turn to friends outside the establishment when they need to discuss any worries, although young people interviewed in England were less likely to turn to 'outside' friends (21 percent; n=21) than those in Germany (47 percent; n=55) or Denmark (36 percent; n=31) (see Table 7:1; p<0.001).

We asked the young people about their friendships outside the establishment. Similar proportions in each country said that they had socialized with outside friends during the day and evening over the previous four weeks. More striking differences were to be found in the extent to which friends from outside had visited the establishment during the same period. Bringing friends home is a 'normal' part of social life for many young people who are not in residential care. Among the young people we interviewed about life in residential care, 37 percent (35) in England, 53 percent (60) in Germany and 59 percent (49) in Denmark said a non-resident friend had visited them in their establishment during the day within the past four weeks (p<0.01). Thirty-two percent (31) of young people in England, 22 percent (25) in Germany and 48 percent (40) in Denmark said a non-resident friend had visited them in the establishment during the evening within the past four weeks (p<0.001). Perhaps most strikingly, just one young person interviewed in England (1 percent), compared with 18 percent (18) in Germany and 29 percent (24) in Denmark, said a non-resident friend had stayed overnight in the establishment within the previous four weeks (p<0.001).

To summarize the above findings: young people in Denmark socialized with friends in the residential home more than those in the other two countries. Those in England were the least likely to invite friends home (except for evening visits, where they did so slightly more than was the case for the German young people). It was especially rare for young people in England to have friends stay overnight.

Staying with a friend overnight speaks of a closeness of relationship and mutual liking, and can also be a means of promoting such relationships. An invitation to stay overnight is less casually made, and may be seen as a greater indication of friendship, than an invitation to visit during the day or evening. Staff policy about residents entertaining friends was not pursued in interview, but there was anecdotal evidence that the English homes, at least, viewed this as a risky procedure. These findings may both relate and contribute to the relative isolation of the English children, itself connected to their greater instability of placement. It also means that staff are less aware of residents' social networks and in a weaker position to either support or monitor them. Crouter and colleagues' research on parenting (2005), outlined in Chapter 1, suggested that parental knowledge of young people's everyday lives is protective for young people, and associated with lower rates of high risk behaviour such as drug or alcohol use or criminal offending. Familiarity with a young person's friends would seem a key part of such 'everyday knowledge', but this may be difficult for a residential care worker (or a parent) to achieve if the young person is unwilling or unable to bring their friends home.

Discussion

The words of the young people interviewed for this study paint a mixed picture. We catch sight of difficult, edgy environments with staff who, from the young people's perspective, can be somewhat capricious and with fellow residents who are not entirely to be trusted. At the same time, young people appreciate staff and the effect they can have on their lives; by and large they see them as a source of support. Some of their verbatim reports convey a warm appreciation for staff. Most residents, also, enjoy activities with their peers, although only around a quarter would turn to another resident if they had a problem.

Over all, it would seem fair to say that, based on their own accounts, the residential experience of the young people interviewed in England was more disadvantaged and more socially excluding than that of their counterparts in the other two countries. In many ways, residential care seemed to be more favourable for young people in Denmark, while the accounts of those interviewed in Germany often revealed an intermediate position between the other two countries.

For example, young people in England whose placements were of shorter duration than for the other two countries were rather less inclined than the others to advise a new resident to approach staff for advice. Their accounts indicated greater social exclusion and disadvantage. They reported less involvement and less satisfaction regarding the ways in which decisions were made about day-to-day activities. They gave evidence of less contact with members of their family: they went on holiday with them less often than the residents in the other two countries; fewer English young people said that they would turn to a family member if something was worrying them, and they did not refer to staff 'making a difference' in terms of their relationships with family members. They went on holiday less frequently, and were more likely to report that they had not been on holiday at all during the last year, compared to the children in the other countries. They said that they enjoyed group activities and activities with members of staff slightly more frequently than the children interviewed in Germany, but less frequently than those interviewed in Denmark. Fewer of them spoke of enjoying skills or creative activities with staff and none said that they enjoyed doing homework with staff, compared to the handful of residents in Germany and Denmark who, unprompted, said they enjoyed doing homework with their pedagogues. In one striking respect the English establishments were less 'home-like' than those in Germany or Denmark: friends visited young people less often and having a friend to stay overnight was very rare.

Residents in Denmark, on the other hand, painted a more favourable picture, less redolent of social exclusion and disadvantage. While between country differences did not always reach statistical significant, there was a consistent pattern across almost all questions, with young people in Denmark offering more positive replies than those in Germany and England.[4] They provided evidence that they enjoyed themselves more than their counterparts in England and Germany. Nearly all of them (84–87 percent) enjoyed group activities and activities with staff. When they were asked about what they liked doing with staff, they reported more, and more varied, activities. In answer to the same question, almost half of them spontaneously mentioned enjoying companionship with staff.

The high value placed on young people's collective life is evident in many of the Danish findings. Residents in Danish children's homes spoke in terms of cosiness and enjoying time together indoors, of outings and sports and physical activities, more than the others. Again, almost all of them (92 percent) had been on group holidays with others in their establishment – more than their counterparts in Germany and England. Indeed, they had holidayed more frequently than the others, and all the young people interviewed in Denmark had taken a holiday during the previous year. They were also more likely to have friends visit them, including for overnight stays, than residents in the other two countries. In this respect, they were less excluded from 'normal life' than the English children especially.

Turning to the ways in which young people could influence their everyday lives, around three-quarters of those interviewed in Denmark found the means at their disposal – from formal meetings to informal conversations – satisfactory, and they reported more ways of taking part in decision-making than the others: social participation appears to have been more of a reality for those in Denmark than was the case in England or Germany. More young people in Denmark would advise a new resident to speak to a member of staff about any difficulties that they experienced than in the other countries and, alongside this sign of confidence in staff, they also reported significantly more sources of support than did young people in England.

As we have said, the accounts of the young people in Germany mostly fell somewhere between those of young people in England and those in Denmark. They had more holidays than young people living in English children's homes, but fewer than those in Danish homes. More of them, than young people in England, would turn to a family member for support, but fewer would do so compared to young people in Denmark. They reported fewer ways of participating in decision-making than young people in Denmark, but more than English young people, and so on. Exceptionally, they were more likely to turn to a non-resident friend if they had a problem than young people in the other two countries. They were also somewhat less likely than young people in England to say that they enjoyed group activities within the establishment, and activities with staff.

How should we interpret these between country differences? They are important because they speak of differences in the quality of life of young people in residential care in the three countries. The relatively favourable position of children in residential care in Denmark may, in part, relate to the Danish universal approach to welfare and to the value placed on social participation and equality. It is this system, also, that provides residential care with a highly qualified workforce. The different national profiles with regard to training and qualification would seem to predict, for many findings, the advantages of Danish residential care, the frequent middle positioning for German care and the more often disadvantaged English position.

Notes

1   Ranked scores were compared across countries using a Kruskall-Wallis test.
2   Kruskall-Wallis test.
3   For each item, we awarded a score of one for every reply that could be classified as positive, and zero for a non-positive (negative or ambivalent) response. These dichotomous scores were then summed to give an overall positive score for the grouped items. The same method was employed for calculating a mixed/ambivalent sum (each item scored zero for a positive or negative response and one for a mixed/ambivalent response) and for the negative sum (each item with a negative response scored one, all those with positive or ambivalent responses scored zero). The range of possible scores for these summary variables were as follows: 0 to 11 for the positive sum; 0 to 10 for the mixed/ambivalent sum; and 0 to 12 for the negative sum.
4   All cross-country differences referred to in this concluding discussion are statistically significant.

8 Three English residential homes

The studies described in this book were undertaken in order to explore what continental European understandings of social pedagogy, and the role of the pedagogue, might have to offer in the future development of English policy and practice. So far we have shown that, in many ways, English establishments seemed to provide less favourable conditions for young people in care. Furthermore, while conditions in German establishments appeared to be less positive than those in Denmark, differences between the two countries were often in line with the proportion of staff in each who had a higher or lower level of qualification.

Earlier in the book, we described pedagogy as an approach to work with children that is based in 'education in the broadest sense'. One point of view often voiced when we have presented the research findings to knowledgeable English audiences is that this approach is similar to that found in good residential care in England. We believe there is merit in examining the ways in which some establishments in England appear to be doing better than others, and to acknowledge their work in supporting the development and well-being of looked-after children. To this end, we considered all 25 of the English homes included in the study and asked ourselves whether they were pursuing a broadly pedagogic approach. That is, for each candidate home, we looked at several areas that could be said to be important for children's current, and possibly future, well-being.

For each establishment, we examined any policy and practice designed to foster children's achievement and to ensure their attendance at school or other educational establishment. We also considered whether the staff approach to young people's difficulties regarding school and education was broadly positive and constructive. Subsequently, we considered the proportion of young people out of education or employment altogether, and what, if any, daily activities were arranged for this group. Next, we considered emotional support for young people provided by staff and whether there was a focus on establishing positive relationships between staff and young people. Finally, we evaluated whether the home encouraged young people to take up, or continue, a 'normal' social life, including friendships with non-resident peers. On this basis, seven of the 25 English establishments were identified as having a 'pedagogic' orientation, in that their practice could be construed in terms of a commitment to *education in the broadest sense*. The remainder focused more on the *management* of young people and their behaviour or, in the case of four homes, provided a mixed picture of inconsistent accounts from different members of staff.

On this basis, this chapter presents case studies of three residential homes in England, situated in different parts of England. For each home, we shall seek to draw out the characteristics that, we believe, provide examples of practice more akin to pedagogic methods. We draw on the reports of manager's, staff and young people, and the informal observations recorded by ourselves as researchers.

Green Street

'Green Street' was a local authority semi-independent living facility in London. At the time we visited, it had five residents and eight members of staff. Its main function was to offer a transitional period between residential care and life as an independent adult. The home occupied an end-of-terrace house, on three floors, and had no obvious signs of being a children's home from the outside. Inside the décor was bright, welcoming and did not appear to be 'institutional'.

'Individuality' was a key theme in the organization of the home. Each young person had their own food cupboard and lockable fridge and had to do their own shopping. There were five bedrooms, one for each resident, and a sixth for a staff member on night duty. Researchers described a 'warm friendly atmosphere'. When we arrived, a young woman was cooking her lunch in the kitchen. She greeted her key worker with a kiss when the latter came on shift.

The head of Green Street was a qualified social worker, while the two staff interviewed both held qualifications for working with very young children (NNEB and BTEC) and the NVQ Level 3, Working with Children and Young People. One also held a City and Guilds Grade 2 Care Management. Both were female: one had seven years' experience and identified herself as coming from a Black African background; the other had 20 years' experience and came from a White Irish background. The average annual pre-tax salary earned by these two members of staff was £18,880, well below both the London average salary (£36,022) and the national average (£25,170) (Bulman 2003).

The head of establishment said he was proud of two things. The first was to have changed the local reputation of the unit so that placements were looked upon as a positive option for young people. This had entailed ensuring that the local 'key players' (council members and senior staff in the local authority social services department) were aware of the unit's recent successes in preparing young people for independent life.

The second successful outcome that he identified was to have given the young people 'a kind of a voice'. This had meant eliciting young people's views about daily life in the establishment and garnering their ideas about what they required from social and other services. One of the primary avenues for this work was the key worker. In meetings between key workers and residents, the focus was on the young people's own perspectives as well as what was expected of them as a resident. The head said: 'Once you get the relationship right, you can really move them on ... [it's] based on equality and mutual trust ... when they see they can have some influence over their lives [they are] much more confident and [you] can move them from A to B'.

This focus on relationships was supported by our observation of one of the staff we interviewed who was described as an 'extremely warm, lively, Black African residential social worker. She was very enthusiastic about her work, and appeared to be popular with the young people'. The researcher observed her engaged in active caring and attentive relations with residents, for example, advising a girl to 'wrap up' because it was cold, and to take medicine for a head cold, encouraging her about school work and showing interest in the mock examinations she was taking. In response, the girl hugged the worker spontaneously before she left to take the exam.

However, not all workers in the home were so positive about the job: a second respondent was far less enthusiastic about what she saw as a lack of effectiveness in residential placements and expressed some doubts about the motivation of some staff, who were described as doing the job 'for the money, not because they want to work with young people or feel committed'. She hoped that introducing a mandatory qualification (NVQ Level 3) would change this, although she was concerned that becoming qualified would accelerate the process of staff leaving residential care for other types of social care work.

Unsurprisingly, these two members of staff had different perspectives on the positive aspects of the job: the first valued the occasions when 'advice gets through and you can see them move on', and when young people acknowledged that they had moved on, perhaps after leaving the home. The second worker could see few positive aspects of the job at the time of interview, because, she said, positive outcomes were not always easy to identify.

These two staff members assessed themselves as feeling settled at Green Street. Its small size generated an intimacy between staff and residents that allowed staff to know what was going on most of the time. They liked the resulting ethos of the home and the greater chance to develop constructive relations with the young people. Staff saw their work as 'in-depth' practice rather than 'babysitting' (as one described her role at a previous establishment). The ethos of the establishment was seen as one likely to attract more experienced staff.

Both members of staff saw themselves continuing to work with young people. One was working towards qualifying as a social worker, and running her own small home as a sort of hybrid fostering/residential care. The other was less certain, but saw herself working in a family centre or homelessness advice centre.

The head of establishment argued that investment in staff practice and self-development was critical for successful staff retention. He said that retaining staff was dependent on building and supporting teamwork: not always easy in what he called a policy climate of 'acute change'. He did not see this change as necessarily negative: some change, such as the emphasis on acquiring an NVQ qualification, was important in giving staff direction in their work, so 'staff don't get sucked into the young people's behaviour' – meaning, perhaps, that greater professionalization helped staff to maintain appropriate distance from the young people and the ability to act in young people's interests, rather than being overwhelmed by the difficulties young people sometime presented.

The head also believed that retaining the establishment's autonomy to refuse or accept referrals for admission was essential. This helped to preserve the practice focus on the particular client group likely to benefit from the Green Street regime – rather than take in 'inappropriate admissions', young people likely to undermine the ethos he wished to promote.

He referred to external support for himself and the staff as an important factor in Green Street's success. He had access to support and guidance for the staff group, and for individual young people from a local psychiatric service. There was also support from a designated teacher who helped to engage young people in education and skills training. The head said: 'We try to push education here, [the] only way out of poverty is skills and education'.

The residents at Green Street were from mixed ethnic backgrounds: three white British or Irish, one from a mixed white and black Caribbean and the other of Caribbean ethnicity. From the young people's perspective, the staff had made a positive difference to their lives and they believed that residents were treated with respect. One young man said, 'They have given me a lot of help that has really made a difference to me. Helped me to get on with my life and move onto independence, so I can get my own flat. They teach us how to manage and give us suggestions to try out'.

All five of the residents said that the staff were mostly good at listening to the residents' points of view, in spite of not always agreeing with the views the young people expressed. A young woman said, 'They're good at listening but, because they are older and more experienced, I get the impression they feel they know best. I understand that, but it can be frustrating – being put in a category'. The young people thought that most of the staff were fun to be with, most of the time, although caveats were mentioned: 'Sometimes, you [they] can be in a grumpy mood, anyone can'. Overall, the residents rated the staff performance very highly: a young woman said that the staff 'work really hard to look after the young people here . . . it's a lot better here than where I was before . . . here I have staff to talk to and feel a lot safer'.

The defining characteristics of this provision were its small size, homely environment and an investment in social relations that appeared to result in trust and respect among the staff group and between staff and residents. Also important was the sense of integrity and identity the home retained through controlling its own admissions. (However, from an outside perspective, this policy could have an adverse knock-on effect for other residential establishments and for foster care and, therefore, ultimately for the population of young people in the public care.)

Heather Grove

'Heather Grove' was a local authority long-stay children's home for six girls and one baby, in the North Midlands area of England. Most girls and young women stayed for at least three years, or until leaving care around the age of 18. Heather Grove had a warm relaxed atmosphere, which was described as coming to life 'when the girls arrive back in the afternoon'. Researchers noted a lot of noise, shouting and people hanging around. The kitchen was described as the 'hub' of Heather Grove, with girls gathering around the cook, who prepares a main meal in the evenings in term time and at lunchtime during the holidays.

In the dining room there was one long table, where everyone ate together and 'it's a sociable time between staff and girls' wrote the researcher. There was a large garden and an open spacious feel to the building. The office was not accessible to the girls, but was located by the main entrance, and there was lots of activity around it.

The head had been in post for five years and held qualifications in social work, and youth and community work, as well as NVQ Level 3 and the NVQ assessors' award. The head liked to think of Heather Grove as providing positive placements for young women and not as a last resort. She thought young people sometimes 'preferred this to foster care as they feel [fostering] can't replace their own family. I'd like to banish stereotypes of children's homes – this is not a naughty girls' home [that] they have been banished to. We work very well in partnership with other agencies and that is very important for best outcomes for young people'.

What we have described throughout this book as a relational approach, more typical of pedagogy, was indicated by the head's interactive and affectionate style with the residents. She was described, by the researcher, as 'very approachable, very proud of the home and how good it is', and of how stable the staff were. She thought the home was sought after because it was for girls only. For some girls and young women, this was a good placement where they could be 'relieved of bothering with boys' and could talk freely. Of the 20 staff members, two were male. One of them, whom the researcher met (but did not interview) said that Heather Grove was an open and friendly establishment, where physical affection and emotional reassurance were given through, for example, hugging and kissing between staff and residents. This male member of staff expressed some concern about how physical affection could be interpreted but, at the time of interview, there had been no examples of 'girlish crushes' on him, nor allegations of impropriety.

The residents of Heather Grove were expected to attend school. This was in order to foster their self-esteem and to provide opportunities for friendships and a sense of a 'normal' existence. School attendance was supported through personal education plans for each resident drawn up in conjunction with schools, and through staff attending school meetings and award ceremonies with, or instead of, parents. There was close liaison between key workers and designated teachers in school, in order to avert difficulties and to keep young people in school. Young people were given incentives for attendance and for dealing with any difficulties that might arise. Staff ensured that residents were ready for school each day with all the equipment needed, having eaten a good breakfast. On arriving back at Heather Grove after school, the head said staff gave girls the opportunity to talk about their day 'as part of normal life'. Further education was encouraged; the head said: 'it's important young people are not seen as different from others on courses … we prepare them for further education, get them up in the morning, make it as smooth as possible'.

Relations with neighbours and the local community were also said to be good, helped by regular meetings to discuss common issues. Residents usually took part in local events.

The manager was proud of the way young people liked living in the establishment, they felt safe and benefited from good team working relations among the staff group. She described the staff as giving 110 percent to working with children. There was a minimal use of casual staff and low rates of sickness among staff.

The two staff members interviewed, both of whom held an NVQ Level 3 Caring for Children and Young People and one of whom in addition held local youth and community work qualifications, were described by the researchers as enthusiastic and thoughtful. The average annual pre-tax salary earned by the two members of staff interviewed was £19,024 at the time of fieldwork.

One worker focused on the developmental progress of residents as a source of satisfaction, but also mentioned her own role: 'watching child become comfortable here and learn to trust us, and me being part of the process'. This way of describing the staff role is akin to the pedagogic notion of 'being with' a young person, where there is a consciousness about social relationships as a basis for change and growth.

In response to questions about practice, one of the two staff members focused mainly on risk assessment, and less on the role of emotional support.

She believed that one of the most positive aspects of the work was through continuing contact with residents after they had left.

Both members of staff felt settled in their work, and both referred to the same positive qualities of the work environment that had been mentioned by the head. They said they enjoyed the age group they worked with, they had good support from the staff team and through regular supervision sessions, they had approachable management and one of them specifically praised the working conditions at Heather Grove.

For the future, one staff member was planning to retire in two years time, while the other would stay in the field of work with children and young people; she saw herself staying where she was for the next five years. Both would recommend their work to a friend.

Four of the five residents interviewed thought staff were 'mostly good' at talking things through or listening when young people had something on their mind. One young woman differed from this view point, saying that she had told staff for the last six months I am not happy here and want to move out and nothing's changed. The unit's too big; it's like a youth club, people walk in and out all day. [I] would like a smaller place ... more like a family, but not part of someone else's family [as] I have my own.

The other girls thought the staff very good at listening to their point of view and gave examples from the girls' fortnightly meeting with staff. One said, 'They listen to your viewpoint and compromise with you', giving as an example a discussion about the prospective admission of a young mother and her baby, and the impact of this change on the other residents. One young woman said the staff did their jobs 'brilliantly, every single one of them'. Another concurred that the staff at Heather Grove let her 'do things I want to and that's better for me, [it was] way unreasonable at home'.

Overall, the characteristics of Heather Grove that most impressed were the emphasis on 'normal' life, and the focus on constructive social relations, such as interaction and affection, that this emphasis requires to take effect. The interpretation of normal at Heather Grove also included a focus on participation and achievement in education, and a participative approach to social relations with the wider community.

Lilac Park

'Lilac Park' was a privately run, long-stay establishment in the north of England, based in an old country house with comfortable furnishings of a high standard with, the researcher noted, few 'institutional touches'. There were eight residents and 19 staff members. Lilac Park had a clearly defined therapeutic objective, based on psychodynamic principles. Staff spoke in terms of the inner world of the child being both a source of distress *and* of strength, from which positive changes could develop. The head, in post for 17 years, had qualifications in residential care, counselling and management in social services.

The establishment included an educational unit with facilities for art, pottery, photography, gymnastics, learning resources and play therapy. Staff and young people made extensive use of the outdoors, including taking holidays together and local bike riding. As with other establishments selected as having a broadly 'pedagogic' orientation, the researcher noted much evidence of warmth and physical affection between adults and children. For example, when the researcher complimented a young person on her cooking 'in front of a large male member of staff, they both laughed and he gave her a proper big hug'. The head of establishment talked of trying to do what a good parent does, and this accorded with the researcher's informal observations.

There was much emphasis on the resources of 'the group' working together, the group of young people and the staff team. Both met together on a daily and weekly basis for 'community meetings'. For the weekly meetings, young people, supported by staff, set the agenda. These community meetings were held the day before staff meetings, where matters arising from them were discussed. Staff had an obligation to report back the results of the staff discussion at the next daily meeting with residents.

Integration into local services and community were positively encouraged at Lilac Park. There was a high expectation that residents would attend school, partly to ensure educational success and partly to give residents the opportunity to have friends outside Lilac Park. An internally appointed education coordinator visited schools weekly and supported residents in school lessons.

The importance given to education was such that local authorities had to commit to paying for 25 hours per week home tuition for the young people whom they placed, until a school placement was found. Moreover, and exceptionally for English residential care, the head of house reported that virtually all the residents continued into further education after compulsory schooling finished. The head saw herself as working in partnership with all the local schools attended by residents, and the head of one local junior school was a trustee of Lilac Park. The head also took active steps to involve residents in the local community through taking part in the local carnival, fete and sporting events.

Retaining staff was said to be not difficult because of their enjoyment of and commitment to the work, which had a 'depth and breadth to it'. The head said 'we are not about warehousing young people'.

Up to six staff were on duty at any one time, which enabled support to always be available to residents. The head maintained an open door policy, which in practice meant that lockable doors were propped open. The head saw herself as available for staff, but not as constantly supervising staff practice. External support was available through psychodynamic consultants and through the local Child and Adolescent Mental Health team.

The two staff members interviewed had university degrees (one in art therapy). In addition to their degrees, one of them had NVQs at Levels 2 (Working with Children and Families with Learning Difficulties) and 3 (Caring for Children and Young People) and training in counselling and anger management. Average annual pre-tax staff salary was low, at £15,702, about £7000 below the regional norm (Bulman 2003).

One staff informant said she felt settled at work due to 'really good support' that made staff feel they are 'being heard, valued and supported', although both informants recognized that the work was stressful, and that teamwork could often be difficult. Both would recommend their work to a friend and saw themselves in residential or related work with young people in five years time.

The five residents interviewed agreed that the staff had made a positive difference for their lives. One young man said that the staff had 'sorted me out quite a lot. My behaviour used to be really bad but now I'm much better, although I'm still up and down sometimes'. Four of the five residents said the staff treated them with respect; the fifth gave a more reserved judgement, saying that 'some of them do', and singled out his key worker as someone who 'listens to everything and doesn't interrupt'. Other examples of respect that the young people provided were being fed adequately, being given privacy, reciprocal listening between staff and residents, staff dealing actively with difficult situations that arose between residents, and staff being able to preserve confidentiality.

All young people interviewed thought staff were 'mostly good' at listening to them, with regular opportunities for young people to contribute to decisions about daily life through the residents' meetings. Staff were rated by young people as doing their jobs well or very well, and residents recognized that it's a 'really hard' job and the staff are 'very, very nice people'.

A striking characteristic of Lilac Park was the coherence of its approach, based in an explicitly therapeutic framework, and its consistent use of the whole group, staff and residents, as a resource and as a means of reciprocal accountability.

Discussion

In each of the above case studies, we have tried to draw out the features of some English establishments that came closest to the ethos and practice of pedagogy. We have focused on the physical environment, the social relations between adults and children, the way young people's skills and participation in daily life are valued and the extent to which children's integration in the local community is fostered. The views put forward by staff contribute to an evaluation of the head's report as to the ethos of the establishment and how it is managed. The views of young people offer a commentary on the social environment they inhabit. We have chosen these three homes because they seemed to represent most vividly the homes based on more pedagogical values and practice. All had a clear sense of purpose about what they were trying to do. All emphasized the importance of a relational approach, with a comfortable degree of physical warmth and affection between children and staff, alongside clearly articulated boundaries and expectations about daily life. Staff encouraged young people to take up further and higher education. Integration into the local community through education and local friendships were other common features. Staff in these homes seemed able to employ a variety of empathic and discursive emotional support strategies in work with young people. Although this has not been discussed in the case studies, they also produced fuller responses to the researcher's vignettes about real life situations than many other English respondents, which may indicate an ability to reflect on, and articulate, their working practices.

These case studies, and our research overall, support the findings of Sinclair and Gibbs' earlier study of residential care (1998), which indicated that both leadership and vision are required in order to achieve effective children's homes. In the same study, Sinclair and Gibbs found that high level qualifications play a minimal part in achieving successful homes, and in the three homes described above, staff qualifications were not particularly high. Nevertheless, throughout the preceding chapters, in comparing English establishments with their continental counterparts, we have found them less adequate. Looked at comparatively, English residential care appears to lack a *coherent* educational base from which to judge the effect of worker's qualifications (if any): their background qualifications are too varied as to content and level. This lack of a coherent background makes it less likely that staff and heads of establishment can share a common vision and common understandings: a perhaps greater problem in establishments where there is a high turnover of staff, as was the case for the English establishments in comparison with the others. With high staff turnover there is less opportunity to develop a common vision.

We would also argue that leaders and workers must have *adequate* professional knowledge and confidence to negotiate daily group life with severely disadvantaged young people. They should be equipped, not only with strategies, such as how to include young people in decisions, listen to them and take account of their views, but also with a sufficient level of theory to know why they are doing so and how they may do it better. They also need a professional ethos that recognizes the value of respecting the young people in their care. These are professional underpinnings which, in the pedagogic tradition, support staff in both negotiating young people's sometimes challenging behaviour, and in having sufficient confidence and self-knowledge to enter affectionate social relationships with them. Pedagogues are children's companions in daily life *and* they have to get children to go to school and do their homework. The educational under-achievement of English looked-after children has many causes, but it is something that staff can, as we have seen from these case studies, address. The question of warmth and affection between adults and children in English residential homes remains a difficult one that has not been fully resolved in policy (Cameron 2004) and is haunted by the spectre of abuse of residents (Kendrick 1998; Barter 2003).

Placement options

The three 'pedagogic' establishments presented above lead us to the consideration of placement options for looked-after children. Compared, for example, to Denmark, Germany, France and the Netherlands, England, as we saw in Chapter 3, has a higher proportion of children in foster care than in residential care. In England, there has been a deliberate policy preference for fostering. This preference has several causes, including problems with the quality of care provided in large institutions, the high cost of keeping children in these establishments and recent scandals about child abuse. Importantly, foster care is generally seen as approximating more closely to a 'normal' upbringing than is possible in an institutional placement. It may also make for greater social integration within the local community and be less stigmatizing.

While some might suggest that an ideal position would be for all children to be looked after in family settings, in fact the number of foster placements in England is, at the time of writing, insufficient. Furthermore, fostering may not meet the needs of all children. There have been good reasons to distrust residential care, but perhaps there are equally good reasons to question its position as a residual service for difficult-to-place young people. Some respondents in England spoke in terms of a residential service that had been 'run down' locally, a 'Cinderella' service, while at the same time being very expensive. A better way forward might be to develop the potential strengths of residential care: it is likely to remain a placement option for children in care. It does not have to be of poor quality. And the continental pedagogic model is not necessarily more expensive. In fact, staff salaries (converted to purchasing power parity ratings) were no higher in Germany or Denmark than in England, and while the present study did not include an economic analysis, the lower staff to child ratios and the fewer reported recruitment and retention difficulties in these countries suggest that staff costs overall are probably lower than in England. Furthermore, the potential costs of social exclusion (e.g., SEU 2004) for looked-after children should serve as a powerful driver for investment in staff education, if this is in turn associated with better 'life chances' for young people in residential care.

As the case studies that we have presented demonstrate, residential care in England can provide 'education in its broadest sense' and be a means of integrating young people with society. Our research leads us to suggest that adopting the pedagogic model, on the basis of a fully trained professional workforce, could point the way forward to a more hopeful future for residential care throughout the UK.

PART 3
Conclusion

9   Extending 'pedagogy'

In our first chapter, we alluded to Worning's telling comment that welfare policy is not 'a distant theoretical abstraction. On the contrary, it can be felt in the body every day' (Worning 2002: 2). In other words, the ways in which public authorities construct and conceptualize social policies have an effect on the physical, mental and emotional lives of the population as a whole, as well as having more specific effects on different sectors of the population. We believe that, in this book, by comparing different national policies towards children in public care, we have shown something of the truth of Worning's statement.

In the preceding chapters we have focused on the contribution that can be made by a particular way of thinking about social policy towards children and young people in residential care: namely a pedagogic approach to work with children. Across different European contexts, we found that pedagogic theory and practice could be drawn on for many of the policy areas that concern children and young people. Yet, while in continental Europe pedagogy may be a broad concept, in English usage the term has little currency outside formal education. It is a term that is rarely applied to fields such as residential care, youth work or school age childcare. In this final chapter, we will argue the benefits of extending the connotations of pedagogy to take in broader policy and practice concerns. Our studies indicate that, from the perspectives of policy, theory, practice and ethics, pedagogy is too useful a concept to be confined within the boundaries of the classroom and teaching.

Nevertheless, it must be acknowledged that the terms *pedagogy* and *pedagogues* remain stumbling blocks. They can sound unnecessarily learned or mystifying for English ears. Alternatives, such as 'social educator' and 'social education' have already been adopted in some sectors: for example within social work by British academics affiliated to FESET (the Federation of European Social Education Trainers) whose continental European membership consists largely of people engaged in the training of what they themselves would call pedagogues or *éducateurs*. That said, social education may also be problematic, suggesting more formal education in, for example, areas such as citizenship. Yet, whatever the apparent strangeness of 'pedagogy', this may not in itself prove a long-standing difficulty. People can quickly become accustomed to new terms. Indeed a word such as pedagogy, whose meaning is not immediately apparent, could in time lead policy makers, service providers, educators and practitioners to a fresh appraisal of what is required for work in the children's sector.

We believe that the findings we have presented in this book indicate that any difficulties associated with the application of pedagogic theory and practice to work with children and young people are far outweighed by its potential benefits. Pedagogy has the potential for an inclusive, normalizing approach. It relates to a field of study and of practice whose main focus is on children as children: this is one of the many ways in which it is an appropriate basis for fostering social inclusion for disadvantaged children. At the same time, pedagogic theory and practice addresses the fact that children can have special and additional needs. In this respect, also, they can serve to promote greater social inclusion and coherence. Pedagogy as a theory is also implicitly relational, and draws on theories of upbringing and attachment. In this holistic conceptualization of the relationship between worker and child, a pedagogic education perhaps prepares the worker to balance professionality and caregiving in a way that competency based qualifications cannot.

In the course of this book we have examined policy and practice towards one particular group of children and young people at risk of social exclusion, and have seen that the pedagogic approach appeared to be more likely to promote their greater social integration, both currently and for their future social benefit.

In Denmark and Germany, more often than in England, staff set out to provide young people with the resources for social integration, and did so on the basis of coherent values, understandings and practice. The primary vehicle for supporting such an integrationist approach towards young people was pedagogy, in the particular professional approach of the pedagogue and the way in which staff related to young people. A pedagogic establishment is one which builds on both individual and collective relationships to supports the holistic development of children and young people. Staff bring themselves as persons to their work and see young people as fellow human beings, individuals with qualities and strengths, with whom to share many aspects of everyday life. These include routine events as well as the enjoyment of play, companionship and creative activities.

We have spoken throughout the preceding chapters about the importance of warm relationships, based in attachment and mutual enjoyment, as protective for young people. By this, we do not mean that care staff should be parent substitutes or that they should think of themselves as parents, but that they should be 'good-enough carers'. That is, that they should aim to build relationships based on trust and mutual enjoyment, using the activities of daily life as the medium for their work, relationships that – to adopt the language of attachment theory – allow young people in residential care to conceive themselves as valued and competent, with carers who are perceived to be emotionally available, but also as supportive of engagement in the wider world.

In England, recent government guidance (DfES 2005: 8, 12) addresses the need of all children and young people to be supported by warm relationships and speaks of

> the importance of being special to someone, being able to express feelings, develop healthy dependence' and of 'ensuring the ... young person's requirements for secure, stable and affectionate relationships with significant adults, with appropriate sensitivity and responsiveness to the ... young person's needs

The emphasis of this guidance is clearly informed by theories of parenting and attachment such as those we have discussed in the preceding chapters. Should not these same qualities also be central to a young person's relationship with staff, who are among the significant adults in their lives? If so, our research suggests that a pedagogic approach may promote these qualities and can address young people's relationship needs.

Let us take one further aspect of staff practice: whether or not staff reported that they would respond to a child's problems by physically comforting them. Lack of direct human physical contact may be a great deprivation for children and young people. The willingness of pedagogues to provide physical contact and cuddles speaks of the professional confidence of staff and of the confidence that their employers have in them. It also relates to principles of seeing the child as a whole person, rather than the more distant and organizational approach that was typical of English responses.

We also saw that a feature of pedagogic practice was the ability to be empathic and non-directive when providing emotional support for young people: listening, spending additional time with them, accompanying them in difficult circumstances, giving them positive affirmation. These descriptions of practice accord with the pedagogic concept, derived from psychoanalytic theory, of *rummelighed*, (meaning literally, space, capacity), implying the capacity to accept others, because of self-knowledge, an awareness of one's own reactions and the dimensions of one's own personality which may resonate with those of the other person. This is not to say that pedagogues neglected to provide more structured guidance to young people, but we found that they could and did combine both approaches.

In all the continental European countries that we studied, a fairly lengthy initial training underpins the holistic, relational and reflective approach. This is a training which recognizes that engaging the self, on a daily basis, with sometimes challenging young people calls for both personal and professional resources. These resources include the ability to turn to, and reflect on, the theoretical and ethical foundations of the work. No less important is the knowledge that other members of the staff team share similar professional understandings. A pedagogic establishment is one which supports the holistic development of children and young people, where staff bring themselves as persons to their work and see young people as fellow human beings, persons with qualities and strengths.

While pedagogy and a pedagogic approach would appear to have much to offer, we should remember that pedagogy is not value-free. Indeed, in furthering social inclusion and integration, pedagogies promote the dominant values of the society in which they exist. They aim at 'producing' a certain type of person, and a certain ideal of society. To take some contrasting examples: the Soviet Pioneer Movement was one type of pedagogic approach, as were the settlements of Robert Owen and the *Sure Start* initiative in England today. Earlier (Chapter 2), we raised the question of whether pedagogy is seen as serving emancipatory ends or relates more closely to systems of social control. This is a subject that also exercises pedagogic thinkers in other European countries. According to the Nordic Forum for Social Educators:

> ... social educational [pedagogic] objectives have changed from the education, re-socialisation, and normalisation towards activation, self-determination, and life quality ... In reality, however, integration is not a matter of either adjustment [of the individual to society] or liberation. It is a process that includes both aspects. The readjusting aspects of integration imply that the participants acquire norms and routines that are the general consensus in society. This acquisition of culture also comprises an aspect of liberation, because when the individual masters the fundamental norms of actions in the community ... this will increase his/her options ... [in] such a way that a transgression of cultural norms and routines happens on the basis of the conscious choice, as an action based on qualified decision made by the individual.
>
> (NFFS 2003: 8, 9)

In other words, the pedagogic approach, when it is informed by democratic values, allows for conscientious dissent.

In all the countries in continental Europe that we studied, the pedagogy employed with children in residential homes was aiming at the 'self-determination', 'liberation' *and* the 'social adjustment' of which the NFFS document speaks. Pedagogic practice provided a means by which, at a daily level, there was space for the child's voice to be heard and for children to learn to negotiate with one another and with adults. The models and values upon which pedagogues built were broadly those of democracy and citizenship: children and young people were drawn into these. Pedagogy is, after all, what Payne (2005) refers to as a 'reflexive' practice, in which all participants are seen as affecting each other and as affecting those processes in which they are jointly involved.

Pedagogic practice is directly linked to understandings derived from the theoretical and ethical considerations that underpin the profession of pedagogy. These are considerations that exist somewhat separately from the domain of public policy, although they interact with it. Ethical and theoretical considerations have their development in various professional bodies, in pedagogues' experience and daily practice, and in the pedagogic research and analysis conducted in the universities. As we remarked at the beginning of this book, the term pedagogy, as used in much of continental Europe, relates to an organic system of thought, policy and practice that applies to many areas of work with children and young people. It is the richness of the concept that, for us, demands its extension beyond the purely educational connotations that are, typically, to be found in English language and thought. An extended definition of pedagogy provides a foundational concept for policy and for training the children's workforce for employment in and across children's services. As such, it has great potential benefit for children's and young people's lives and social well-being – not least for children and young people in residential care.

Appendix: Design and methods

Study 1

A comparative case study approach was used to explore pedagogic training and practice in five European countries. Belgium (specifically, Flanders), Denmark, France, Germany and the Netherlands were selected to provide diverse examples of residential settings and approaches. For each country, a combination of approaches was used, including the perusal of reports and other documents, and interviews with key informants. It was also decided to expand the scope of the study to obtain the views of some key English informants on what the pedagogic approach might have to offer to the English residential care system. This was achieved via interviews, seminar discussions and a small scale survey of colleges and universities.

Documentation

In Belgium, Denmark, France and Germany a national expert was commissioned to provide a written overview of residential child care, occupational standards and pedagogic training. In the Netherlands, this report was confined to an overview of residential child care. Other relevant documentation was collected during the course of fieldwork visits to each country, and translated by national experts or by members of the research team.

Interviews

The establishments selected for the study were identified by local experts as providing good examples of the pedagogic approach, judged against national criteria. The interviews achieved are shown in Table Appendix 1.

Face-to-face interviews were conducted with:

- Staff and students in pedagogic training centres. The staff interviewed included the head of department, or equivalent, and staff engaged in teaching and supervising students directly. Students were

chosen by staff on a variety of grounds including, for example, their availability and, where necessary, their facility in speaking English.
- Staff in children's residential facilities. The head of establishment and at least one member of staff who worked directly with the children.
- National and, where appropriate, regional officials with responsibility for residential care and/or workers' training.

Many informants spoke English but interpreters were used during interviews where necessary. Many of the Dutch and German interviews were conducted in these languages by the research team, as were all French interviews. Depending on local circumstances, in-depth interviews were carried out individually where possible and, occasionally, with two or more informants. Students in training colleges were interviewed in groups. Virtually all interviews were tape recorded for reference and most were transcribed. Numbers of interviews conducted varied across countries for local reasons. For example, it was deemed appropriate to interview only one civil servant in Flanders – reflecting the size of the Flemish community and the allocation of responsibility for looked-after children in that country. In Germany, with a far larger population and a federal system of government, three civil servants were interviewed.

Interview topics

To ensure comparability across countries, interviews followed topic guides, as outlined below.

Civil servants

Individual professional background and responsibilities; policy objectives regarding training and qualifications; national and regional policy for residential facilities (development and implementation); values and aims for training or residential care; legislative requirements for care provision and staff training in residential facilities; views on the pedagogic approach.

Heads of residential establishment

Length of time at establishment and as head of establishment, professional background, responsibilities; type of establishment, name and designation in own language, literal translation thereof, description of premises, number of children, sex, ages, any with disabilities/difficulties, any subject to youth

Table Appendix 1: Participants Study 1

Country	Interviews undertaken
Belgium (*Flanders*[1])	
Policy:	Civil servant, Ministry of the Flemish Community, Brussels
Training:	Department of Orthopedagogics, University of Ghent
	Head of Department; placement tutor; group meeting and discussion with students.
	Department of Social Agogy, University of Ghent
	Head of Department
	ISPOC Hoge School (KATHO), Kortrijk
	International coordinator; placement tutor; students' focus group
Residential care:	Wagenschot Pedagogical Centre, Eke-Nazareth
	Director; orthopedagogue; focus group with residents
	Centrum voor Integrale Begeleiding (CIB), Roeselare
	Director; orthopedagogue; residents focus group
Denmark	
Policy:	Civil servant, Ministry of Social Affairs, Copenhagen
	Head of regional department dealing with service provision for children (health, education and welfare); Head of section with responsibility for mental handicap.
Training:	Social Pedagogic Seminarium, Copenhagen
	Rector of Seminarium; international coordinator; lecturer; students' focus group.
	Jydskpedagogic Seminarium, Aarhus
	Deputy Head of Seminarium; placement supervisor; two focus groups.
Residential care:	Dalgaardens Behandlingshjem, Aarhus
	Head of establishment; social pedagogue; residents focus group
	Solhaven, Farso
	Head of establishment; social pedagogic consultant; residents' focus group
France[2]	
Policy:	Interview with Chair of national association of residential care providers and of college principals
Training:	BUC Ressources Ecole d'Educateurs Specialisés, Versailles
	College principal.
Residential care:	Foyer Départmental de L'enfance de Villepinte, Saint Denis
	Director of establishment; informal interviews with educateurs and other staff on site.
	Maison d' Enfants à Caractère Social Les Marroniers, Versailles
	Director of establishment

Germany[3]

Policy:	Civil servant, Federal Ministry for Family Affairs, Senior Citizens, Women and Youth; Deputy director Landesjugendamt (State Youth Service); Administrative Head of Health Youth and Social Matters, Landkreis
Training:	Institute for Social Pedagogy, University of Lüneberg: Head of Social Pedagogy degree course; social pedagogy tutor; students' focus group with 6 students. Faculty of Social Pedagogy, Fachhochschule, Hamburg Two professors in the faculty; discussion with class of 14 students. Alsterdorf Fachschule fur Heilerziehung, Hamburg Head of school and the subject area School, Children and Youth Assistance; Director of Welfare Care and Education course; three members of teaching staff; student focus group.
Residential care:	Stadtteil Milieunahe Erziehungschilfe (SME), Hamburg Head of establishment; two betreuer; residents' focus group. Margaretenhort, Harburg Head and Deputy Head of establishment; four betreuer; residents' focus group

The Netherlands

Policy:	Chairman of the national steering group for youth care (Landelijk Platform Jeugdzorg; former member of the national committee for pedagogy training, current editor of the journal SPH (the professional journal for social pedagogues)
Training:	University of Amsterdam, Professor of Orthopedagogics University of Leiden, Two professors- Social pedagogy and social policy High School of Amsterdam: one member of staff University of Utrecht: Professor of Orthopedagogics and two pedagogy students High School of Utrecht Group interview with four staff; two student focus groups;
Residential care:	MFO: 2 area managers, 1 pedagogic scientist working in several homes for younger children (4–14); 2 senior workers in a residential home for older children (14–18); residents' focus group

Notes: 1 Flemish and Dutch training in pedagogics distinguish between University *licenciaat* qualifications in orthopedagogics (concerning special needs), social agogics (applicable to the general population), and the *hoge school* vocational diploma in pedagogy. The orthopedagogy licenciaat and the hoge school diploma can both lead to work in residential settings. 2 The term *éducateur specialisé* translates as specialist educator, but – as with pedagogues in other countries in the study – the role incorporates care and upbringing, rather than education in its formal sense. 3 *Fachhochschule* translates as a university of applied sciences. The *fachschule fur Heilerziehung* is a vocational school for welfare care and education. The literal translation of *betreuer* is someone who cares for you or looks after you.

justice procedures; staffing, any resident staff, overnight staffing; main aim for children, policy, practice and any difficulties regarding different minority groups, children's contact with family, schooling, health and use of health services, health records; what is meant by social pedagogy, duties of social pedagogue, contribution to children's daily lives, their status compared with that of teachers, care assistants and psychologists, core values in social pedagogy, any problems or difficulties associated with the social pedagogy approach, how well training fits pedagogues for the work; any other important areas and/or difficulties relating to work with children in a residential establishment not yet raised.

Pedagogues working in residential establishments

Length of time at establishment, professional background, responsibilities; qualification, when and where trained, number of years in training post-secondary education, any residential work prior to training; hours, shifts, children responsible for; daily work: description of last working day and all people/agencies involved, typicality of that day; aspects of work with children that was particularly satisfying or enjoyable/less satisfying or difficult considering last working day/month/year; main aim for children in terms of daily life, long-term aims, most important aspects of work; main aims, practice and any difficulties regarding children's contact with family, schooling, health and use of health services; what informant means by social pedagogy, most important aspect of the social pedagogues' duties, with example, special contribution to children's daily lives, pedagogues as compared to teachers, care assistants and psychologists, core values in social pedagogy, any problems or difficulties associated with the social pedagogy approach, how well training fits pedagogues for the work; professional advantages/disadvantages of work, intentions to remain in work with reasons; any other important areas and/or difficulties relating to work with children in a residential establishment not yet raised.

Heads of college/department of pedagogy

Length of time at establishment, as head of establishment/department, professional background, qualifications, responsibilities, contact with students, number of students and their sex and age range, courses that lead to work with children in residential care, full-time/part-time, duration of course, place of social pedagogy, any practice placements, description of intake for course, entry requirements, proportion of applicants accepted, staffing – including number teach social pedagogy, cost of course and how funded, at what level students have to specify direction of studies, strategies to encourage applicants from ethnic minorities and applicants with disabilities, students' career paths, any discussion of training with policy makers, recent changes in national policy about training, effects on courses, most important aspect of training for work with children in residential establishments, most important skills for staff who work with children in residential care and their development in students, most difficult and most rewarding aspects of training for students, any perceived gaps in the training, meaning of social pedagogy, its core values, contribution to work with children in residential settings, most important aspects of this work; any problems or difficulties associated with the social pedagogy approach, appropriateness of current training for work in residential establishments.

Lecturers in colleges/departments of pedagogy

Length of time at establishment, professional background, qualifications, responsibilities, courses taught, including those leading to work with children in residential care, contact with students; meaning of social pedagogy, its core values, contribution to work with children in residential settings, most important aspects of this work; any problems or difficulties associated with the social pedagogy approach, appropriateness of current training for work in residential establishments; most important elements and skills for training for residential settings; the vignettes used with students (below) were also employed with teaching staff in colleges.

Students

Questionnaire
Students were asked to complete a questionnaire giving: age, gender, ethnicity, name of course and eventual qualification, length of training course, full- or part-time, previous professional qualifications and work experience, work would like to do on completion of course. Two methods were used to trigger discussion on students' understandings of pedagogy and the work of the pedagogue:

Drawings
Students were asked to draw a 'good' social pedagogue and a 'bad' social pedagogue, and then to spend 15 minutes discussing their drawings as a group. What did the 'good' social pedagogues have in common? What did the 'bad' social pedagogues have in common? – What sort of things does each say to a child (insert speech bubbles)? What do they think about the children they work with (insert think bubbles)?

Vignettes

Six vignettes were devised about some situations that may arise in working with children or young people in residential care. Each situation was described in two or three stages, as the scenario developed. For example, one began with a child missing her parent and ended with the child failing to return from a family visit. Others addressed racism and bullying; cigarette, alcohol and drug use; romantic and sexual relationships between residents; school non-attendance; and family contact problems. These were used as trigger material with students and with pedagogues working in residential establishments to elucidate the pedagogic approach. In each case informants were asked what they would do in each situation as it developed.

Additional sources of information that informed the first part of the research included: discussion at two seminars UK, attended by senior civil servants and local government officers, academics in relevant fields and others holding senior positions in voluntary sector organizations; one of these included presentations from Belgian, German, Dutch and Danish colleagues who had written the national reports; interviews with 11 expert informants in England, drawn from similar backgrounds as those who attended the seminar.

A survey by telephone, email and fax of as many English educational establishments providing early years courses, early childhood degrees and social work as we could identify, with 53 responses. We tried to establish whether they were teaching pedagogy or European approaches to social work and residential care, and whether they were interested in developing this approach.

Methods study 2

The second phase of the research comprised a formal comparison, with a mixed quantitative and qualitative design, of residential settings in England, Denmark and Germany. Work in England was conducted by the English research team; fieldwork in Denmark and Germany was conducted by local researchers who had expertise in pedagogy and had been involved in the first phase of comparative research. Two of these national experts (Inge Danielsen and Tim Tausendfreund) also translated the research materials into Danish and German, and these materials were developed through a process of iterative piloting and discussion across all three countries. Originally, it was intended that France should also be included in the study, but the French research associates withdrew at an early stage and it proved impossible to instate a new French team given the timescale and demands of the research.

The sample

In each country, sampling was conducted in three geographic areas: one north, one south and one in a major city (in England, a London borough). Residential homes were selected to represent a wide variety of settings in each country, taking into account the following: different administrative regions, areas of relative disadvantage, small town and inner-city settings, differing sizes of establishment and establishment providers (private for-profit and non-profit, and public sector).

The size of residential homes differed in each country, and consequently the number of residential homes visited also varied, because the study aimed to interview 100 young people in each country. In England, a sample of 100 young people was achieved by visiting 25 homes; in Denmark, the sample comprised 86 young people in 12 establishments; and in Germany, 116 young people were interviewed in 19 residential homes. The need to increase the number of residential homes visited in England led to the extension of the sample to include the adjoining local authority, and/or to homes in which children from the sample authorities were placed.

All heads of establishment were selected for interview (N=55). Four residential care workers were selected in larger establishments, and two in smaller establishments, on the basis of length of service in that setting total (N=138). (For example, where four members of staff were selected, one was selected with more lengthy service, two with medium-length service and one with less experience, with the proviso that staff employed for less than three months should not be sampled). Resident young people (ranging from two to 12 per establishment, total N=302) were also sampled. In larger establishments, children were sampled to represent the age range to be found in that establishment, to provide a fairly equal number of boys and girls and to represent the ethnic mix of the establishment. In all establishments we were restricted to sampling from young people who had themselves consented to be interviewed and whose parents and/or social workers had given consent; in smaller establishments, therefore, we found ourselves interviewing all who had the necessary consent.

Interviews

All interviews were conducted face-to-face, in a quiet room within the residential establishment, to ensure respondents' privacy. For all interviews, open-ended questions followed a structured format, with pre-determined categories to enable concurrent coding of responses by the researcher conducting the interview.

Interviews with managers

We collected summary information about the establishment and provider; young people resident; staffing; respondent's professional background; training and staffing issues (e.g., recruitment and retention); welfare concerns for young people; and management policies and practices in relation to young people's use of health services; education and employment; contact with families and with the local community; transitions to independent living. Managers also completed a short questionnaire which asked about the staff group and recorded data from establishment records about outcome indicators relating to residents from the year 2001.

Interviews with residential care workers (pedagogues)

We collected some summary data about the staff and young people with whom the respondent usually worked, and went on to address participants' perceived roles and responsibilities and day-to-day work with young people, asking about working practices in relation to: young people's health; education; contact with families; emotional support; communication with young people; and residents' decision-making. One section of the interview asked workers to generate suggested strategies for dealing with situations described in three staged vignettes, developed from those used in the first study. These related to family contact, bullying and racial abuse, and drug and alcohol use, and are discussed in more detail in Chapter 5. The final section of the interview addressed workforce issues, including satisfaction with work, training, and future career plans. Staff also completed a short questionnaire that collected some background information (e.g., age, gender, training, working hours).

For interviews with young people

Two age-specific interview versions were created, for use with young people aged 12–14 and those aged 15–18. Interviews with both collected some background information (age, gender, ethnicity, length of placement), along with questions about free time activities; education and employment; use of health services; and views of residential care staff (e.g., in relation to emotional support and decision-making).

Ethical considerations

The research was conducted in accordance with the Ethical Code and Procedures of the Thomas Coram Research Unit and the Institute of Education,

University of London, as well as the requirements of the Data Protection Act (1998). Information sheets on the study were prepared in relevant languages, and written consent was obtained from parents' and young people's social workers where appropriate, as well as from participants themselves. At the end of interviews, participants were asked for their evaluation of the interview and any concerns raised were addressed. The information leaflet provided a contact telephone number so that any further concerns or enquiries could be raised. Care was taken to ensure that all interviews were conducted with the freely given informed consent of participants, and respondents have been anonymized in this report of the work. All participants were informed of their right to refuse to answer any questions and to withdraw from the study at any time without explanation. This information was provided verbally, with the opportunity for questions at each stage of explanation.

Analytic strategy

All data analyses (quantitative and qualitative) were conducted by the English research team, drawing on pre-coded numeric interview data entered into SPSS, and interviewer notes on interview schedules (translated into English where necessary).

Statistical tests offer a probability – the 'p value' – that the result has occurred by chance. In social science, the commonly accepted convention is that where $p < 0.05$ (a 5 percent probability that the result occurred by chance), the finding is taken to be 'statistically significant'. Tests also make a number of assumptions about the data they handle, and those called 'parametric tests', such as analysis of variance and multiple linear regression, are designed on the assumption that the data being analysed are 'normally distributed' (if graphed, data would produce a bell-shaped curve). In fact, in the case of the present study, that was not necessarily the case, because the samples in each country were quite small and participants were not randomly recruited to the study; as has been noted elsewhere, we interviewed all young people who were available and gave their consent to participate, and at least two members of staff who were working at the time of the site visit. While we usually interviewed the majority of residents in an establishment, they may not be representative of those who did not take part in the research, and this is similarly true for the staff sample.

In statistical terms, these factors mean that our analytic strategy (using multiple regression and ANOVA with data that were not normally distributed) may have increased the probability of finding a false positive (a type 1 error): a relationship between variables, or a difference between countries, that has in fact occurred by chance. Given a more conservative approach to analyses, the converse would be true, increasing the likelihood that a finding would be falsely attributed to chance. The present research offers a formative exploration of the implications of pedagogy as an approach to residential care, so it was important that the analytic strategy adopted did not miss subtle relationships between variables or small scale differences between countries. Consequently – while bearing in mind the caveats noted above about the characteristics of the data – it was decided that multiple regression and analysis of variance offered the most appropriate analytic tools for elements of the analysis of this study.

A more detailed account of each stage of the analysis is given within each chapter, as appropriate.

References

Abrahamson, P. (2002) Quo Vadis? The future of the Nordic welfare model, *Nordisk Sosialt Arbeid, Nordic journal of Social Work*, 22(3B): 6–13.

Ainsworth, M.D.S., Blehar, M.C., Walters, E. and Walls, S. (1978) *Patterns of Attachment: A Psychological Study of the Strange Situation*. Hillsdale, NJ: Lawrence Erlbaum.

Bakermans-Kranenburg, M.J., van IJzendoorn, M.H. and Juffer, F. (2003) Less is more: meta-analyses of sensitivity and attachment interventions in early childhood, *Psychological Bulletin*, 129(2): 195–215.

Baldwin, D., Coles, B. and Mitchell, W. (1997) The Formation of an underclass or disparate processes of social exclusion? Evidence from two groupings of 'vulnerable youth', in R. MacDonald (ed.) *Youth, the 'Underclass' and Social Exclusion*. London: Routledge Falmer.

Barber, B.K. (1996) Parental psychological control: revisiting a neglected construct, *Child Development*, 67: 3296–319.

Barnardo's (1996) *The Failure of Social Policy to Meet the Needs of Young People Leaving Care*. Ilford: Barnardo's.

Barter, C. (2003) *Abuse of Children in Residential Care*. Available at http://www.nspcc.org.uk/Inform/OnlineResources/Information Briefings/Abuse of ChildrenInResidentialCare_asp_ifega26011.html (accessed 17 April 2006).

Barter, C. and Renold, E. (2000) 'I wanna tell you a story': exploring the application of vignettes in qualitative research with children and young people, *International Journal of Social Research Methodology*, 3(4): 307–23.

Baumrind, D. (1967) Child care practices anteceding three patterns of preschool behaviour, *Genetic Psychology Monographs*, 75: 43–88.

Beihal, N., Clayden, J., Stein, M. and Wade, J. (1995) *Moving On: Young People and Leaving Care Schemes*. London: HMSO.

Berridge, D. and Brodie, I. (1998) *Children's Homes Revisited*. London: Jessica Kingsley.

Boddy, J., Cameron, C., Heptinstall, H., McQuail, S. and Petrie, P. (2003) Working with children: social pedagogy and residential child care in Europe. Unpublished report to the Department of Health.

Bowlby, J. (1951) Maternal care and mental health, *WHO Monograph Series*, 2. Geneva: World Health Organisation.

Bowlby, J. (1973) *Attachment and Loss: Volume 2. Separation, Anxiety and Anger*. London: Hogarth Press.

Brannen, J., Breckmann, M., Mooney, A. and Statham, J. (forthcoming) *Coming to*

Care: The Work and Family Lives of Workers Caring for Vulnerable Children. Policy Press: Bristol.

Bretherton, I. and Munholland, K.A. (1999) Internal working models in attachment relationships: a construct revisited, in J. Cassidy and P.R. Shaver (eds) *Handbook of Attachment: Theory, Research, and Clinical Applications.* London: Guilford Press.

Briggs, A. (2004) Reversing a spiral of deprivation: working to ameliorate the relationship of staff and boys in a residential home, *Journal of Social Work Practice*, 18(1): 33–48.

Browne, K., Hamilton-Giachritsis, Johnson, R. and Ostergren, M. (2006) Overuse of Institutional Care for children in Europe. British Medical Journal, *332*, 485–487.

Bulman, J. (2003) Patterns of pay: results of the 2003 New Earnings Survey, *Labour Market Trends*, December: 601–12.

Byrne, D. (1999) *Social Exclusion: Issues in Society Series.* Buckingham: Open University Press.

Cameron, C. (2004) Social pedagogy and care: Danish and German practice in young people's residential care, *Journal of Social Work*, 4(2): 133–51.

Cameron, C., Carlisle, J. and Moore, C. (2003) *Barriers to Lifelong Learning in the Care Workforce: A Study of NVQ Training for Social Care Workers in Cambridgeshire.* Cambridge: Cambridgeshire County Council/Learning and Skills Council.

Cannan, C., Berry, L. and Lyons, K. (1992) *Social work and Europe.* Basingstoke: BASW/Macmillan Press.

Care Standards Act (2000) London: HMSO.

Cassidy, J. and Shaver, P.R. (eds) (1999) *Handbook of Attachment: Theory, Research, and Clinical Applications.* London: Guilford Press.

Chambers, H. (2004) *Creative Arts and Play for the Well-being of Looked After Children, Highlight 212.* London: NCB.

Chase, E., Douglas, N., Knight, A., Rivers, K. and Aggleton, P. (2002) *Teenage Pregnancy among Young People looked after by Local Authorities: Determinants and Support for the Mother, Father and Child. A Review of the Literature.* London: Thomas Coram Research Unit, Institute of Education, University of London.

CIPD (Chartered Institute of Personnel and Development) (2004) *Recruitment, Retention and Turnover 2004: A Survey of the UK and Ireland.* Available at: http://www.cipd.co.uk/surveys

Children Act (1989) London: HMSO.

Children (Scotland) Act (1995) London: HMSO.

Colton, M.J. and Hellinckx, W. (1993) *Childcare in the EC: Country-specific Guide to Foster and Residential Care.* Cambridge: University Press.

Cost, Quality and Child Outcomes Study Team (QCOST) (1995) The cost, quality and outcomes study theoretical structure, in S.W. Helburn (ed.) *Cost, Quality and Outcomes in Child Care Centers.* Denver: University of Colorado at Denver.

Courtioux, M., Davies, H., Jones, J. et al. (1986) *The Social Pedagogue in Europe: Living with Others as Profession*. Zurich: FICE.

Crimmens, D. (1998) Training for residential child care workers in Europe: comparing approaches in the Netherlands, Ireland and the United Kingdom, *Social Work Education*, 17(3): 309–19.

CROA (Children's Rights Officers and Advocates) (2000) Strategic plan, *Planning Guidance 2001 for Early Years*. London: Department of Health.

Crouter, A.C. and Head, M.R. (2002) Parental monitoring and knowledge of children, in M.H. Bornstein (ed.) *Handbook of Parenting Volume 3*, 2nd edn. Mahwah, NJ: Lawrence Erlbaum.

Crouter, A.C., Bumpus, M.F., Davis, K.D. and McHale, S.M. (2005) How do parents learn about adolescents' experiences? Implications for parental knowledge and adolescent risky behaviour, *Child Development*, 76(4): 869–82.

Davies Jones, H. (1986) The profession at work in contemporary society, in M. Courtioux, H. Davies, J. Jones et al. (eds) *The Social Pedagogue in Europe: Living with Others as a Profession*. Zurich: FICE.

Department of Health (1989) *An Introduction to the Children Act*. London: HMSO.

Department of Health (1998) *Modernising Social Services*. London: The Stationery Office.

Department of Health (2000) *The Children Act Report 1995–1999*. London: The Stationery Office.

Department of Health (2004) *National Service Framework for Children, Young People and Maternity Services: Core Standards*. London: Department of Health. Available at http://www.dh.gov.uk/assetRoot/04/09/05/66/04090566.pdf (accessed 11 May 2006).

DfES (Department for Education and Skills) (2003) *If This Were My Child. A Councillor's Guide to Being a Good Corporate Parent*. London: Department for Education and Skills. Available at: http://www.dfes.gov.uk/educationprotects//upload/ACFC03E.pdf (accessed 1 Sept. 2005).

DfES (Department for Education and Skills) (2005) *Children's Workforce Strategy: A Strategy to Build a World-Class Workforce for Children and Young People*. Consultation document. London: DfES. Available at http://www.dfes.gov.uk/consultations/downloadableDocs/5958-DfES-ECM.pdf (accessed 11 May 2006).

Dréano, G. (1998) *Guide de l'éducation spécialisée*. Paris: Dunod.

Dréano, G. (2001) Social pedagogy and residential care in France. Unpublished report for the Thomas Coram Research Unit, Institute of Education, University of London.

Esping-Andersen, G. (1990) *The Three Worlds of Welfare Capitalism*. Cambridge: Polity Press.

Esping-Anderson, G. (1999) *Social Foundations of Post-Industrial Economies*. Oxford: Oxford University Press.

Eurodice/Eurostat (2005) *Key Data on Education in Europe 2005*. Luxembourg: Office for Official Publications of the European Communities.

Finch, J. (1987) Research note: the vignette technique in survey research, *Sociology*, 21(1): 105–14.

Gibbs, I. and Sinclair, I. (1998) Private and local authority children's homes: a comparison, *Journal of Adolescence*, 21(5): 517–27.

Goffman, E. (1961) *Asylums: Essays on the Social Situation of Mental Patients and Other Inmates*. New York: Doubleday.

Goffman, E. (1963) Stigma: *Notes on the Management of Spoiled Identity*. Englewoods Cliffs, NJ: Prentice-Hall.

Hämäläinen, J. (2003) The concept of social pedagogy in the field of social work, *Journal of Social Work*, 3: 69–80.

Hatton, K. (2001) Social work in Europe: radical traditions, radical futures? *Social Work in Europe*, 8(1): 32–43.

Higham, P. (2001) Changing practice and an emerging social pedagogue paradigm in England: the role of the personal adviser, *Social Work in Europe*, 8(1): 21–9.

Hill, M. (2000) Inclusiveness in residential care, in M. Chakrabarti and M. Hill (eds) *Residential Child Care*. London: Jessica Kingsley.

Howe, D. (2005) *Child Abuse and Neglect: Attachment, Development and Intervention*. Basingstoke: Palgrave Macmillan.

Howes, C. and Ritchie, S. (1999) Attachment organization in children with difficult life circumstances, *Development and Psychopathology*, 11: 251–68.

Improvement and Development Agency, The (1999) *Independent Sector Children's Residential Homes Survey 1998*. London: Employers' Organisation.

Jackson, S. (1994) Education in Residential Care, *Oxford Review of Education*, 20(3): 277–9.

Jensen, J.J. (2000) Social pedagogy and residential care in Denmark. Unpublished report for The Thomas Coram Research Unit, Institute of Education, University of London.

Jensen, J.J. (2001) *Personal Communication*. Aarhus: Jydsk Pædagog-Seminarium.

Jensen, N.E. and Christiansen, A.W. (2000) How to educate pre-school teachers so they are capable of working with social development of children, CICE Conference paper, Athens, May.

Jensen, J. and Hansen, H. (2003) *Danish National Report for Workpackage 7*: work with young children. Unpublished report for Care Work in Europe, Jydsk Pædagog-Seminarium, Aarhus.

Kendrick, A. (1998) *Abuse of Children in Residential and Foster Care: A Brief Review*. Available at http://www.sircc.strath.ac.uk/research/kendrick.html (accessed 17 April 2006).

Kretchmar, M., Worsham, N. and Swenson, N. (2005) Anna's story: a qualitative analysis of an at-risk mother's experience in an attachment-based foster care program, *Attachment and Human Development*, 7(1): 31–49.

Lorenz, W. (1994) *Social Work in a Changing Europe*. London: Routledge.

Lorenz, W. (1998) The ECSPRESS approach: guiding the social professions between national and global perspectives, in O. Chytil and F.W. Seibel Ostrava (eds) European Dimensions in Training and Practice of Social Professions, Conference Papers ERASMUS – TNP – Conference papers, Ostrava/CZ, August: 26.

Madge, N. (1994) *Children and Residential Care in Europe*. London: NCB European Children's Centre.

Mainey, A. (2003) *Better Than You Think: Staff Morale, Qualifications and Retention in Residential Child Care*. London: National Children's Bureau.

McQuail, S. (2001) Working with children: European models of pedagogy and residential care: Germany. Unpublished report, Thomas Coram Research Unit, Institute of Education, University of London.

Meijvogel, R. and Petrie, P. (1996) *School-Age Childcare in the European Union: A Survey*. London: European Commission Network on Childcare and Other Measures to Reconcile Employment and Family Responsibilities of Men and Women.

Meins, E., Fernyhough, C., Wainwright, R. et al. (2002) Maternal mind-mindedness and attachment security as predictors of Theory of Mind understanding, *Child Development*, 73(6): 1715–26.

Meltzer, H., Lader, D., Corbin, T., Goodman, R. and Ford, T. (2003) *The Mental Health of Young People Looked After by Local Authorities in Scotland*. London: The Stationery Office. Available at www.statistics.gov.uk/downloads/theme_health/Mental=health_Scotland.pdf (accessed 11 May 2006).

Morrow, V. (1999) Conceptualising social capital in relation to the well-being of children and young people: a critical review, *The Sociological Review, 1999*. Oxford: Blackwell Publishers.

Moss, P. and Petrie P. (2002) *From Children's Services to Children's Spaces*. London: Taylor and Francis.

Moss P., Petrie, P. and Poland, G. (1999) *Rethinking School, Some International Comparisons*. Leicester: Youth Work Press.

NFFS (2003) *Nordic Forum for Social Educators*. Copenhagen: NFFS.

National Care Standards for Care Homes for Children and Young People (2000) Edinburgh: Scottish Executive.

National Minimum Standards for Children's Homes (2000) London: HMSO.

National Statistics (2006) *Children Looked After by Local Authorities, Year Ending 31 March 2005*. London: National Statistics.

OECD (Organisation for Economic Co-operation and Development) (2005) *Society at a Glance: OECD Social Indicators 2005 Edition*. Paris: OECD.

Payne, M. (2005) *Theories of Social Work*, 3rd edn. Basingstoke: Palgrave Macmillan.

Percy-Smith, J. (2000) Introduction: the contours of social exclusion, in J. Percy-Smith (ed.) *Policy Responses to Social Exclusion, Towards Inclusion?* Buckingham: Open University Press.

Petrie, P. (2001) The potential of pedagogy/education for work in the children's sector in the UK, *Social Work in Europe*, 8(3): 23–6.

Petrie, P. (2002) Coming to terms with 'pedagogy': reconceptualising work with children, in B. Littlechild and K. Lyons (eds) *Locating the Occupational Space for Social Work: International Perspectives. Expanding Horizons in Social Work and Allied Social Professions Series*. Birmingham: BASW/Venture Press.

Petrie, P. and Simon, A. (2006) Life in residential care: European comparisons, in E. Chase, A. Simon and S. Jackson (eds) *In Care and After: A Positive Perspective*. London: Routledge.

Pettit, G.S., Laird, R.D., Dodge, K.A., Bates, J.E. and Criss, M.M. (2001) Antecedents and behaviour-problem outcomes of parental monitoring and psychological control in early adolescence, *Child Development*, 72: 583–99.

Pringle, K. (1998) *Children and Social Welfare in Europe*. Buckingham: Open University Press.

QCA (Quality and Curriculum Authority) (1999) *Early Years Education, Childcare and Playwork: A Framework of Nationally Accredited Qualifications*. London: QCA.

Rutter, M. and O'Connor, T.G. (1999) Implications of attachment theory for child care policies, in J. Cassidy and P.R. Shaver (eds) *Handbook of Attachment. Theory, Research, and Clinical Applications*. London: Guilford Press.

Simmons, J. and colleagues (2002) *Crime in England and Wales 2001/2002*. London: Home Office. Available at http://www.homeoffice.gov.uk/rds/pdfs2/hosb 702.pdf (accessed 11 May 2006).

Simon, A., Owen, C., Moss, P. and Cameron, C. (2003) *Mapping the Care Workforce: Supporting Joined-up Thinking, Secondary Analysis of the Labour Force Survey for Childcare and Social Care Work, Understanding Children's Social Care Series*. London: Institute of Education.

Sinclair, I. and Gibbs, I. (1998) *Children's Homes: A Study in Diversity*. Chichester: John Wiley and Sons.

Smetana, J.G. and Daddis, C. (2002) Domain-specific antecedents of parental psychological control and monitoring: the role of parenting beliefs and practices, *Child Development*, 73(2): 563–80.

SEU (Social Exclusion Unit) (1998) *Truancy and School Exclusion*. London: SEU.

SEU (Social Exclusion Unit) (1999) *Teenage Pregnancy*. London: Social Exclusion Unit.

SEU (Social Exclusion Unit) (2003) *A Better Education for Children in Care. Social Exclusion Unit Report*. London: SEU.

SEU (Social Exclusion Unit) (2004) *Tackling Social Exclusion: Taking Stock and Looking to the Future Emerging Findings*. London: SEU.

Social Services Inspectorate (1997) *When Leaving Home is Also Leaving Care*. Wetherby: SSI.

Staffordshire County Council (1991) *The Pindown Experience and the Protection of*

Children: The Report of the Staffordshire Child Care Inquiry. Staffordshire County Council.

Stattin, H. and Kerr, M. (2000) Parental monitoring: a re-interpretation, *Child Development*, 71: 1072–85.

Sutton, A. (1991) Deprivation entangled and disentangled, *Journal of Child Psychotherapy*, 17(1): 61–77.

Thomas, G. (2000) Social pedagogy and residential care in France. Unpublished report for the Thomas Coram Research Unit, Institute of Education, University of London.

Titmuss, R. (1958) *Essays on the Welfare State.* London: Allen and Unwin.

TOPSS England (1999) *Draft Training Strategy: Summary Sheet.* Available at: www.topssengland.strategy@ccetsw.org.uk

TOPPS England (2000) *Modernising the Social Care Workforce: The First National Training Strategy for England.* Leeds: TOPSS.

TOPSS UK Partnership 2003 (2003) National Occupational Standards for Managers in Residential Child Care. Available at: http://www.topssengland.net/files/119673_NOS_Booklet_MiRCC.pdf

Tuggener, H. (1986) Social pedagogy as a profession: a historical survey, in M. Courtioux, H. Davies, J. Jones et al. (eds) *The Social Pedagogue in Europe: Living with Others as a Profession.* Zurich: FICE.

Utting, W. (1991) *Children in the Public Care: A Review of Residential Child Care.* London: HMSO.

Van der Ploeg, J.D. and Scholte, E.M. (2001) Residential Child Care in the Netherlands. Unpublished report for the Thomas Coram Research Unit, Institute of Education, University of London.

Van Ewijk, H., Hens, H., Lammersen, G. and Moss, P. (2002) *Mapping of Care Services and the Care Workforce: Consolidated Report.* Nederlands Instituut voor Zorg en Welzijn. Available at: http://144.82.31.4/carework/reports/finalconsolidatedreportwp3.pdf.

Vorria, P., Papaligoura, Z., Dunn, J. et al. (2003) Early experiences and attachment relationships of Greek infants raised in residential group care, *Journal of Child Psychology and Psychiatry*, 44(8): 1208–20.

Waterhouse, S. (1997) *The Organisation of Fostering Services: A Study of Arrangements for Delivery of Fostering Services in England.* London: National Foster Care Association.

Waterhouse, S. (2000) *Lost in Care: Report of the Tribunal of Inquiry into the Abuse of Children in the Care of the Former County Council Areas of Gywedd and Clwyd Since 1974.* London: The Stationery Office.

Whitebook, M., Howes, C. and Phillips, D. (1989) *Who Cares? Child Care Teachers and the Quality of Care in America.* Oakland, CA: The National Child Care Staffing Study.

Winkler, M. (1988) *Eine Theorie der Sozialpädagogik.* Stuttgart: Klett-Cotta.

Winnicott, D. W. (1984) Residential care as therapy, in C. Winnicott, R. Shepherd and M. Davis (eds) *Deprivation and Delinquency*. London: Tavistock Publications.

Worning, A. (2002) The challenges to social work in the Nordic model, *Nordisk Sosialt Arbeid, Nordic Journal of Social Work, 22(3B)*, 2–5.

Index